KU-845-057

The Dependants of the
Coloured Commonwealth Population
of England and Wales

THE DEPENDANTS
OF THE COLOURED COMMONWEALTH POPULATION
OF ENGLAND AND WALES

DAVID EVERSLEY
FRED SUKDEO

LIBRARY · BIRMINGHAM UNIVERSITY

The Institute of Race Relations, London

© Institute of Race Relations 1969

The Institute of Race Relations is an unofficial and non-political body, founded in England in 1958 to encourage and facilitate the study of the relations between races everywhere. The Institute is precluded by the Memorandum and Articles of its incorporation from expressing a corporate view. The opinions expressed in this work are those of the authors.

O

Published by the Institute of Race Relations, London / Distributed by Research Publications, London / Printed in Great Britain by Headley Brothers Ltd 109 Kingsway WC2 and Ashford Kent

Contents

Tables

Tables—*continued*

Appendix Tables

Pyramids, Graphs and Figures

Preface

This brief survey was commissioned from the Social Research Unit of the University of Sussex by the Institute's 'Survey of Race Relations in Britain' in June 1968, and was completed in a period of less than two months. The resources at our disposal in money and manpower were small, and we were unable to use material other than what was readily available from printed sources, supplemented by a number of unpublished reports and calculations derived from the 1967 Notting Hill Housing Survey which the Unit happened to be analysing at the same time. Additionally, we had access to special tabulations from the 1966 10 per cent census that were prepared by the General Register Office for the Institute's 'Survey'. We are therefore grateful for the use of these and the Notting Hill statistics, without which the study could not have been completed. We offer this background in explanation of the production of a piece of work which, given time and money, we should have wished to treat in a different and extended manner.

The bulk of the calculations and their interpretation are the work of Fred Sukdeo, a graduate student in this University, who is mainly engaged on research on the population problems of Guyana. He was assisted by the following: Anna Bassindale, Keith Pearshouse, Elisabeth Ford and James Munnick who edited and prepared the final typed version. Thanks are due to our temporary staff who worked with great energy and enthusiasm to finish the survey in a short time.

Thanks are also due to a colleague of long standing, Valerie Herr (formerly Jackson), now of Berkeley, California, who is a statistical consultant to the 'Survey of Race Relations', and whose presence in England in the final stages of this monograph was of great help to us.

DAVID EVERSLEY

Social Research Unit,
University of Sussex,
July 1968

Chapter 1 / Introduction

In recent years there has been a good deal of public concern about the future size of the coloured Commonwealth immigrant population in the United Kingdom. The 1962 Commonwealth Immigrants Act halted the large inflow of new arrivals which had been observed in the previous two or three years, and the number of new permanent settlers dropped rapidly. There was, in fact, net emigration from the United Kingdom for several years, which was not only caused by more British-born people emigrating, but also by a continuous reflux of recent immigrants to their countries of origin.

We have not examined the position of the other immigrant groups and their dependants, who of course outnumber the entire Commonwealth immigrant group. We can see this from the 1966 10 Per Cent Census, which gave a total of 2,478,060 immigrants living in England and Wales. This figure, which represents 5·26 per cent of the total population of England and Wales, excludes children born in this country. The largest group of immigrants are those from non-commonwealth foreign countries – 837,150 persons; then follow immigrants from coloured Commonwealth countries – 829,750; Irish immigrants, 698,600 and white Commonwealth, 112,560 persons. Thus we see that coloured Commonwealth immigrants represent only one-third of all immigrants and less than 2 per cent of the entire population of England and Wales.

Table 1   Birthplaces of the Whole Population

	Total	Per Cent
Total England and Wales	47135510	100·0
Ireland	698600	1·48
Foreign Countries (excluding Commonwealth)	837150	1·77
Europe	559850	1·19
South Africa	41170	0·08
Other African countries	33890	0·07
United States	88070	0·19
Other American countries	16950	0·04
Asia and Oceania	50620	0·11
U.S.S.R.	47600	0·10
Commonwealth	942310	2·00
White Commonwealth	112560	0·24
Coloured Commonwealth	829750	1·76
Total Immigrants from all countries	2478060	5·26

Source   1966 Census.

1

In the middle sixties, however, the counts made under the Act showed that there was a distinct increase in the number of arrivals in one category — the dependants, those who were entitled to join relatives already in Britain. This, in effect, means wives, and children under 16, though in some cases older children and parents of pensionable age were also entering the country. This caused a certain amount of public alarm, and rather wild guesses were current as to the potential number of further dependants who might join the men already in this country. At the same time, there were rumours about the excessive fertility of immigrants already settled in this country, the rate of illegal immigration, the number of new arrivals who came as students and stayed to work, and other topics.

The projection of the immigrant population as a whole is not an issue here, nor is the fertility of immigrant women in general. However, in attempting to calculate the possible future rates of arrival of people from the Commonwealth, we have had to give some consideration to a number of allied topics.

It may be as well to state here the exact question we have tried to answer:
What is the *maximum* number of coloured Commonwealth immigrants who may be expected to arrive in this country in the next ten years, based on the following assumptions:
(a) that voucher holders will continue to arrive at the same sort of rate as that observed in the last few years;
(b) that the law relating to dependants will not be materially changed and that there is no significant evasion of the regulations, or fraud,
(c) that the immigrants already in this country, or expected to arrive, are not likely to differ very much, in the demographic sense, from their compatriots at home or in other countries of immigration;
(d) that those who arrived here without their families will, subject to the limitations imposed by the regulations, wish to be re-united with them here;
(e) that there is no further significant reflux to the country of origin.

The emphasis must be that we have estimated for the *maximum*, because in actual fact these assumptions are somewhat unrealistic. Employment opportunities in this country have not been growing at a sufficient rate to make it certain that vouchers will be granted even at the rate of the last few years; and in any case they may be given largely to those highly skilled groups who are most likely to return to their own country eventually. Similarly, the observed reflux to countries of origin may accelerate, especially if there is sufficient economic development in those areas to provide increased employment opportunities for skilled workers. Housing difficulties, discrimination, and deflationary measures may all combine to make continued residence in this country less attractive for the immigrants.

Secondly, the assumption of demographic behaviour similar to that in the country of origin is highly unrealistic. On the evidence we present, it is quite clear that the coloured Commonwealth immigrant population here stays unmarried much longer than it does in its home territories, and that many men do not marry at all. It is also clear that there is much more fertility restriction, and that the 'normal' family size of five live children which we assume in much of this report is very unlikely to be reached. Furthermore, the Notting Hill Survey, which may not, of course relate to an entirely typical population, does not lead us to believe that large families are more usual among immigrants than among British-born people of the same age and socio-economic groups.

Thirdly, the assumption that all those who are over here and who are married will be joined eventually by their dependants may be equally unrealistic. As time passes since the big wave of immigration before 1962, more and more of the children left behind will become too old to be allowed into the United Kingdom as dependants. Aged parents eligible to come over, and who are still fit enough to do so, will become more rare. And if, say, a Pakistani has been here for six years without his wife, it is no more likely that he will bring her over in the next six years than that he will himself return home, or that separation will continue indefinitely.

Fourthly, as regards those who are now single (of whom, as we show, there are a very large number), they may do one of five things, only one of which can enter into our 'maximum immigration' calculations. They may stay single, they may marry someone British (or other foreign) born, they may marry a single person of their own nationality who is already here, they may return home or migrate to another country, or they may bring in a spouse under the relevant provision 'others for long-term settlement', that is, those who are not yet dependants or have vouchers but who are permitted to enter, in this case, on personal grounds. Any calculation therefore, which allows for one additional arrival here for each single person present will be rather on the high side.

On the other hand, we also have to make allowance for under-enumeration. It has been demonstrated that the total number of immigrants (especially Pakistanis) who were enumerated in the 1966 census is considerably below the figure calculated from the 1961 census (itself subject to error) plus the known arrivals in the intermediate quinquennium.

We have made some calculations regarding this under-enumeration, and it appears from these that those who gave their birthplace as India are much less deficient in numbers than those who mentioned Pakistan. It may well be that the explanation lies in the fact that many who are Pakistanis by nationality at the moment of entry were in fact born in what was then, and is now, India: in fact there is some evidence for the presence of many migrants from Hindu territories in 1948 among the immigrants here.

Under-enumeration among immigrants from the Caribbean may be partly due to a wrong classification of the actual country of birth. The Notting Hill Survey shows that nearly 10 per cent of these immigrants indicated their place of birth as the West Indies, which is not a country.

So one might average out the under-enumeration of the different national groups and arrive at some overall estimate of the deficiency, but in the absence of detailed survey material this would be dangerous.

The bulk of this report is concerned with the future arrivals of coloured Commonwealth dependants, the ethnic age, marital status and sex composition of those who arrived in this country between the passing of the Commonwealth Immigrants Act and the end of 1967. This is because it is the group about whom we know most, and because we believe that future movement inwards in relation to earlier immigrant groups is likely to become steadily less important.* We have, of course, taken into consideration the defective family structure of those who were enumerated in 1961, and of those rather larger groups about whom we know so little – the arrivals between April 1961 and mid-1962. We do not believe, however, that the flow of dependants relating to these arrivals of six or more years ago will continue at a high rate. Wiles**, on limited evidence, has shown that the average length of separation between parents and children is five years. We have some evidence that the mean age of the immigrants has been somewhere near 30 years for a long time (we are speaking of the male heads of actual or potential households). A man aged 30 who arrived in 1962 from South East Asia would, by 1967, be unable to bring over his oldest child who would have reached the age limit. This is based on the assumption that the mean age of a father was 19 years when his first child was born.

Admittedly, in theory, younger children may continue to arrive throughout the early seventies, but under present legislation only if the mother comes as well, and whilst we have little evidence about the changes over time in the mean length of separation, there seems little reason to suppose that many more of the pre-1962 arrivals will now want to bring over their wives and families. Yet we have made an allowance for the possibility that they might still do so, for those ethnic groups where incomplete families are still prevalent.

The report is not concerned with the demographic future of the immigrants as a whole. We make no allowance for mortality, though increasingly the older immigrants will show significant losses through death so that they cannot bring in potential dependants. We have made no assumptions regarding the possibility that those who were children in 1961, or have arrived since then, will, when they grow up, not marry other immigrants already here, but bring over spouses from their country of origin. In time, those born here, and who do not figure at all in our birthplace tables, and may not do so in the nationality tables if they claim British citizenship, will be eligible to apply for citizens of Commonwealth countries to join them here for the purpose of a marriage arranged by correspondence. They may one day affect the total numbers of 'coloured' people here; but they are not our business at the present time.

One last assumption should be stated. We have throughout taken figures at their face value, whether they came from official sources like the censuses, or the immigration officers, or from *ad hoc* surveys by local authorities, or the Institute's 'Survey of Race Relations in Britain'. Where there have been inconsistencies, we have tried to

---

* The Home Office has estimated that 16 per cent of dependants arriving in 1968 are joining men who arrived before the Commonwealth Immigrants Act, 1962.
** Silvaine Wiles, 'Children from Overseas', in Institute of Race Relations *News Letter* (June 1968), p. 245.

reconcile them, and invariably by an upwards revision, assuming the lower figure to indicate under-enumeration.

However, it is still possible that there is such general evasion of registration, that there have been so many illegal immigrants, that *ad hoc* surveys have not caught those who have eluded the official series, that in the end we are still seriously out on our estimates on total immigrants. But we should need independent evidence of a reliable character before we would believe this. All we can say about our own figures is that we believe them to reflect all that is known, that they are not now seriously inconsistent with each other, and that a projection of future arrivals from them on maximum assumptions has produced the largest possible figure of arrivals in the next ten years. We ourselves believe that the actual number of arrivals will be very much less than this maximum.

We have not attempted any annual breakdown of these arrivals. Our figures refer to a rough ten-year period: how they will be distributed over this period we have no means of guessing. No doubt, short-term changes in economic conditions both here and in the country of origin will have an important bearing on the timing of arrivals. Moreover, changes in the political climate and the implementation of new acts and administrative measures may influence future trends.

Chapter 2 / Growth of the Coloured Population

Twenty years ago, the first batch of immigrants arrived from the West Indies. Since then, immigrants from many Commonwealth countries have arrived here on an organized scale. Various estimates have been made to determine the number of coloured immigrants and their dependants. Some of the figures published are controversial, since the authors have not publicly released their method of analysis.

This study intends to bring the discussion about the number of coloured immigrants under scrutiny, so that future debates may be both on numbers and methods of analysis. We are providing extensive tables and appendices so that the reader himself may be able to perform his own calculations should he so desire.

Recent studies have defined certain demographic characteristics of the immigrant communities. They were sample surveys which were concerned with economic and social problems, on the whole; no attempt has been made, as yet, to examine the immigrant population on a national scale.

These estimates are for the next ten years, and are on maximum assumptions. In our discussion we shall mainly be concerned with the following groups of countries: India,

Pakistan, Jamaica, the rest of the Caribbean (including Guyana), Commonwealth
West Africa (Nigeria, Gambia, Ghana and Sierra Leone), and Cyprus. (Although
Cypriots are often not included within the grouping 'coloured Commonwealth', for
the purposes of our estimates we have included them.) These six groupings of countries
comprised 589,700 persons, or 81 per cent of all coloured Commonwealth immigrants
in 1966. Immigrants from other countries including Malta were estimated to be
138,000 persons in 1966. All these remaining countries are a small proportion of the
total coloured immigrant population who can all be aggregated as the 'rest of the
coloured Commonwealth countries'. They would represent 19 per cent of the total
coloured Commonwealth population in 1966.

The Profile Method of Analysis

The traditional techniques of demographic analysis to determine fertility and family
size were found to be inadequate in a study of this kind. We have to consider that
the immigrant population is continuously moving towards a stable structure: this
takes several years, if indeed such a structure ever comes about.

The actual arrivals in any given year cannot be extrapolated from trends in the past
arrivals of immigrants. For certain groups, such as the Pakistanis, there was a sudden
inflow of female dependants within the last few years which was unpredictable, and is
still difficult to account for. In 1967, Pakistani women dependant arrivals increased
from 2,944 in the previous year to 4,555. Moreover, the number of children
doubled from 6,210 to 12,664 during the same period. No assumptions about a
'normal' period of years of separation between husband and wife are possible, and
therefore, no projection of arrivals on an annual basis can be made.

In the case of the West Indian population, other complications in applying traditional
techniques of analysis emerge. For example, there is evidence to show that the
'consensual union' system which is common in the West Indies has undergone
extensive changes in this country.

Furthermore, the Indian population of Britain contains an element of Anglo-Indians,
people mainly of European descent formerly permanently domiciled in India and who
took Indian (or Pakistani) nationality in 1948 (see p. 9). Their family structure
differs from that of the Indians and we ought to omit them from our calculations.

The age of marriage can be estimated from information in the countries of origin, but
fertility is dependent on the length of continuous marital union. Also, there is the
question of the reflux of immigrants, for whom there is inadequate data especially as
regards their family size, their age structure and re-emigration motives.

To overcome these difficulties, we have used a different approach. This is based on
the profile method of demographic analysis, and assumes a basic family size for each
fertile age group. We assume for the purposes of a maximum estimate that at the
end of the married female's child-bearing life (44 years), her mean number of
children is five. Divided into quinquennial age groups – 19 years to 44 years – the

number of children achieved within each age group is as follows:

Under 19 years	1 child	
19 - 24	„	2·5 children
25 - 29	„	3·5 „
30 -34	„	4 „
35 - 39	„	4·5 „
40 - 44	„	5 „

Given the age structure of married males and females, we can therefore determine the number of children and family size of a given immigrant population. We modify this method when we know the socio-economic structure of each category of immigrants.

We have some detailed census material on the immigrant population in 1966. Though it has limitations we have used this information to shed light on the family structure of immigrants at that date. Some families enumerated at that date will be completely resident in England and Wales, while others will be fragmented, some members in the host country and some still in their home countries. The number of persons from these fragmented families who are entitled to come to Britain to re-form a family may be estimated from a careful analysis of the 1966 census. For example, we can calculate the number of married immigrants who do not have their wives with them in 1966, and we have similarly estimated the number of families who do not have all their children with them in the host country at that date.

Sources

The last two census publications of England and Wales* and the annual Commonwealth Immigrants Act Statistics** provided the basic data for this study. However, these documents themselves are subject to inaccuracies. There are also limitations in using, for example, the 1961 census reports, because in the full count there are few detailed tabulations for demographic analysis. This problem, however, may be resolved by applying the 10 per cent count of the 1961 census, although this is grossly under-enumerated. We shall discuss this aspect of the census in another section of the report.

In addition to the existing published tabulations of the 1966 10 per cent census, which the General Register Office has estimated to be 1.8 per cent under-enumerated for the entire population, we obtained four special tables made available to the Survey of Race Relations, relating to two areas, the Midlands and Greater London Conurbations, which contain information on age structure, conjugal condition, size of household and place of birth. Unless stated, the white Indian and white Pakistani population are included in all tables based on these tabulations.

---

* *Census 1961, England and Wales* (London, H.M.S.O., 1966); *Ten per cent Sample Census, 1966* (London, H.M.S.O., 1968).
** *Commonwealth Immigration Act, Statistics for 1962-7* (London, H.M.S.O., 1967).

The Commonwealth Immigrants Acts provide us with statistics from July 1962 to the end of 1967. We have used the inflow table to determine the arrival of immigrants and their dependants.

Besides these official documents we have supplemented our information from other publications such as: the General Register Office's reports; documents from the Institute's Survey of Race Relations in Britain'; the 1967 Notting Hill Housing Survey, and studies of immigrant populations in their country of origin. (See page 85 for the complete list of references.)

Increase in Coloured Commonwealth Immigrant Population

The coloured population is made up of coloured Commonwealth immigrants and children born to them in England and Wales. According to the 1951 Census of England and Wales, there were 103,000 coloured immigrants from all Commonwealth countries. More than 50 per cent were then from India, Cyprus and Malta. Ten years later the combined coloured population had increased four times to 414,700, among whom Jamaicans alone were 25 per cent.

The net inward flow of coloured Commonwealth immigrants was estimated to be 42,700 in 1955. In the next four years the number of arrivals fell to 21,600, but suddenly in 1960 it increased to 57,700. The largest contingent of Commonwealth coloured immigrants arrived in 1961. They then numbered 136,400, which is almost equal to the aggregate net arrivals for the period 1956-9. Immigration from Commonwealth countries to the United Kingdom was checked by migration controls in July 1962.

Figure 1.
Population Growth of Immigrants in England and Wales from Selected Commonwealth Countries.

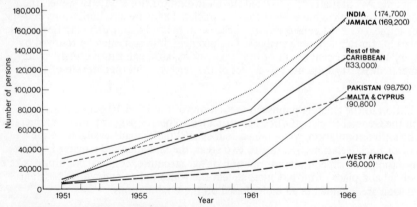

Notes: 1. Figures for 1951 and 1961 are from census reports.
   2. Except for West Africa, the 1966 figures included persons under-enumerated in the 1966 10 per cent sample census.
   3. Anglo-Indians are not included in the immigrant population of India and Pakistan in 1966 estimates.

This rapid increase was intended to be halted by the passing of the 1962 Commonwealth Immigrants Act. Nevertheless, the coloured Commonwealth immigrant population increased by a further 75·2 per cent during the intercensal period, 1961-6. A significant proportion of this increase occurred between the 1961 census and the passing of the Commonwealth Immigrants Act.

Table 2 shows that East African immigrants have nearly trebled during the five-year period; Pakistanis have increased by 175 per cent, and Indians by 79·4 per cent. A very lage number of immigrants have also arrived from Guyana, Nigeria, Singapore, Trinidad and Tobago. We are of the opinion that among the arrivals from the new Commonwealth countries, a significant proportion were white, especially among those from East Africa. Derived from the 1966 census, the countries with the largest coloured immigrant populations in England and Wales were as follows:

India	158,200
Jamaica	151,800
Rest of Caribbean	116,000
Pakistan	68,500

Table 2. Commonwealth Natives in England and Wales, by Place of Birth, from 1951-66*

	1951	1961	1966	% increase 1961-6
*India	30800	81400	158200	94·3
*Pakistan	5000	24900	68500	175·1
Jamaica	6400	100100	151800	51·6
Rest of Caribbean	8900	71700	116000	61·8
C'wealth West Africa	5600	19800	36000	81·8
C'wealth East Africa	3900	10600	31300	195·3
Cyprus and Malta	24700	66600	90800	36·3
Ceylon	5800	9000	12900	43·3
Hong Kong and Malaysia	12000	29900	47000	57·2
Estimate of Total Coloured	103100	414700	742500	79·4
Commonwealth Total	336400	659800	924300	40·0

* This figure excludes white persons from these countries.
Source Population Censuses, and 'Survey of Race Relations in Britain'.

We have excluded the whites in the enumerated population in England and Wales. Their numbers are shown in Table 3.

*See p. 56 for totals at the end of 1967.

Table 3. White Persons in the enumerated Population of Indian and Pakistani Origin

	India	Pakistan	Total Persons
1951	79000	7000	86000
1961	76000	6000	82000
1966	68600	5000	73600

Source Survey of Race Relations in Britain.

According to calculations derived from the 10 per cent 1966 Sample Census, the enumerated coloured Commonwealth population in Scotland was 22,920 persons. This represents only 0·44 per cent of the total population of 5·17 million, as compared with 1·5 per cent (726,500) of the total population of England and Wales (47·14 million). In the composition of the coloured population in Scotland, immigrants from India account for 35·3 per cent, Africa and Pakistan 20·7 per cent and 8·9 per cent respectively. The largest concentration of immigrants is in the Central Clydeside conurbation.

Preparing Tables for Analysis

(a) The 1961 Census

The under-enumeration of coloured Commonwealth immigrants according to the 1961 Census has been discussed by Peach, Hill, Davison and others.* The 10 per cent sample shows a total of 25,484 persons in the six conurbations, whereas the full count shows a total of 308,770 persons; this means that the 10 per cent sample was approximately 17 per cent under-enumerated. This varied with the immigrant groups, but for the Pakistanis, the under-enumeration was 27 per cent, for the rest of the Caribbean 25 per cent and for the Indians 7 per cent. Table 4a shows the under-enumeration of the six conurbations for each immigrant group. Table 4b shows the details for each conurbation for all the immigration groups combined.

---

* G. C. K. Peach, 'Under-enumeration of West Indians in the 1961 Census', in *Sociological Review*, Vol. XIV, No. 1 (March 1966); C. S. Hill, *West Indian Migrants and the London Churches* (London, Oxford University Press for the Institute of Race Relations, 1963); R. B. Davison, 'The Distribution of Immigrant Groups in London', in *Race*, Vol. V, No. 2 (October 1963).

Table 4a.   1961 Census of England and Wales: Actual Sample Size (%) of 10 per cent
Sample as compared to full Count, for different Birthplace Groups, by
Sex, for six Conurbations combined

| | Jamaica | | | Rest of British Caribbean | | |
	Total	Male	Female	Total	Male	Female
Full count	80285	44581	35704	55254	31204	24050
10 per cent sample	6307	3477	2830	4144	2353	1791
Actual Sample size per cent	7·86	7·80	7·93	7·50	7·54	7·45
Per cent under-enumerated	21·4	22·50	20·70	25·00	24·60	25·50

	India			Pakistan		
Full count	82449	47254	35195	20933	18346	2587
10 per cent sample	7653	4116	3537	1535	1287	248
Actual Sample size per cent	9·28	8·71	10·05*	7·33	7·02	9·59*
Per cent under-enumerated	7·20	12·90	0·50	26·70	29·80	4·10

	Africa (excluding Union of South Africa)			Cyprus and Malta		
Full count	24789	16292	8497	45060	25008	20052
10 per cent sample	2158	1408	750	3687	2046	1641
Actual sample size per cent	8·71	8·64	8·83	8·18	8·18	8·18
Per cent under-enumerated	12·90	13·60	11·70	18·20	18·20	1·8·20

* Denotes deviation from 10 per cent sample NOT statistically significant.

Source   Full count figures from Birthplace and Nationality Tables, Table 2; 10 per cent sample
figures from Commonwealth Immigrants in the Conurbations, Table A.2; quoted from P. Jenner
and B. G. Cohen's unpublished paper, 'Commonwealth Immigrants and the 1961 Census (10 per
cent Sample) — Some Problems in Analysis'.

The official explanation of under-enumeration was given by the Registrar General's
Office as follows:

> The cause of this underestimation is not known with certainty but may
> have been due to the following aspect of sample selection. The census
> enumerators were required to deliver the special census form used for the
> 10 per cent sample to every tenth address on their list. It is possible that
> faced with a household where a larger questionnaire would have caused
> difficulties, the enumerator may sometimes have transferred the sample
> census form to another address. The bias thus introduced was generally
> small for most aspects of census data but was more pronounced for
> Commonwealth immigrants. However, the proportional distribution in this
> smaller total, of the various population characteristics, is probably not
> unduly affected.

Table 4b.   1961 Census of England and Wales: Actual Sample Size (%) of 10 per cent
Sample as compared to full Count for each Conurbation, by Sex, for
Commonwealth Immigrant Groups combined*

	Total	Tyneside Male	Female	Total	West Yorkshire Male	Female
Full count	2900	1960	940	15679	11635	4044
10 per cent sample	237	165	72	1210	875	335
Actual sample size per cent	8·17	8·42	7·66	7·72	7·52	8·28
Per cent under-enumerated	18·30	15·80	23·40	22·80	24·80	17·20

	Total	South-East Lancashire Male	Female	Total	Merseyside Male	Female
Full count	13989	8691	5207	5239	3583	1656
10 per cent sample	1108	663	445	545	345	200
Actual sample size per cent	7·97	7·63	8·55	10·40**	9·63**	12·08
Per cent under-enumerated	20·30	23·70	14·50	−4·00	3·7	−20·80

		West Midlands			London	
Full count	45493	30548	14945	225561	126268	99293
10 per cent sample	3065	1982	1083	19319	10657	8662
Actual sample size per cent	6·74	6·49	7·25	8·56	8·44	8·72
Per cent under-enumerated	32·60	35·10	27·50	14·40	15·60	12·80

 * Those Commonwealth groups enumerated in Commonwealth Immigrants in the conurbations,
   that is, persons born in Jamaica, rest of British Caribbean, India, Pakistan, Africa (excluding
   Union of South Africa), Cyprus and Malta.
** Denotes deviation from 10 per cent sample NOT statistically significant.

Source   Full count figures from Birthplace and Nationality Tables, Table 2. 10 per cent sample
figures from Commonwealth Immigrants in the Conurbations, Table A1; quoted from Jenner and
Cohen, op. cit.

There may be other reasons, such as the non-random selection of the 10 per cent
sample, and the use of a sample of households rather than of people.

(b) *The 1966 Census*
The first four tables, obtained from the Survey's special tabulations, were originally
divided into two parts, the centre and remainder of the two conurbations – Greater
London and the Midlands. Knowing the population of the six conurbations, and
given the population of the two conurbations, we have determined the detailed

information for the six conurbations. The two conurbations — Greater London and the Midlands — represent the following proportion of the six conurbations:

Table 5.   Proportion of Coloured Commonwealth Immigrants in London and Midlands to six Conurbations

Country of Origin	Total	Male	Female
India	82·8	81·4	84·6
Pakistan	61·5	61·3	62·4
Jamaica	90·0	88·7	91·0
Rest of Caribbean	89·9	89·1	90·8
Africa	85·6	83·4	89·4
Cyprus	96·4	96·5	95·5

Source   1966 Census.

These calculations were based upon the figures of the Report of the Registrar General's Office, Table 6, birthplace of the whole population. Having obtained the 'structural upgrading' of the six conurbations from the two, we determined the population of England and Wales using the same principle. Table 6 shows the proportion of the six conurbations to England and Wales. We can also ascertain the structural upgrading of the entire immigrant population by a direct increase from the two conurbations to England and Wales (see Table 6).

Table 6.   Proportion of Coloured Commonwealth Immigrants in six Conurbations to Total Population in England and Wales.

Country of Origin	Total	Male	Female
India	55·7	58·7	54·2
Pakistan	67·3	68·3	61·7
Jamaica	79·4	77·8	79·7
Rest of Caribbean	76·9	77·5	76·3
Africa	78·8	80·0	76·7
Cyprus	82·0	82·0	82·3

Source   Special Tabulations from 1966 Sample Census for London and West Midland Conurbations upgraded for England and Wales.*

* This source is referred to subsequently as Special Tabulations.

Table 7. Dependants of Coloured Commonwealth Immigrants 1962-7 by total Persons, Men, Women and Children and Territories
Index 1963 = 100

	India		Pakistan		Jamaica		Rest of Caribbean		Cyprus		C'wealth West Africa		Group of six Territories		Remainder of Coloured Commonwealth		Total Coloured Commonwealth	
	No.	Index	No.	Index	No.	Index	No.	Index	No.	Index	No.	Index	No.	Index	No.	Index	No.	Index
Total:																		
1962	1565	–	505	–	2570	–	1160	–	438	–	886	–	7124	–	1096	–	8220	–
1963	6616	100	3304	100	5522	100	2374	100	1063	100	2292	100	21171	100	3288	100	24459	100
1964	8770	133	7046	213	7877	143	3584	151	1750	165	2492	109	31519	149	4219	128	35738	146
1965	12798	193	6763	205	7480	135	3667	154	1128	106	2452	107	34288	163	4940	150	39228	160
1966	13357	201	9319	282	6622	120	3254	137	587	55	1882	82	35023	165	4107	125	39130	159
1967	15822	239	17506	530	7872	141	3339	141	505	48	1103	48	46147	217	3936	120	50083	205
Total	60127		44443		37943		17378		5471		11107		175272		21586		196858	
Men:																		
1962	46	–	12	–	87	–	37	–	17	–	15	–	214	–	21	–	235	–
1963	235	100	139	100	150	100	83	100	55	100	29	100	691	100	82	100	773	100
1964	329	140	241	177	230	153	108	130	107	194	39	135	1054	153	132	160	1186	153
1965	502	214	204	147	216	144	129	155	91	165	36	124	1178	170	241	294	1419	184
1966	856	364	165	119	71	47	52	63	39	71	24	83	1207	175	120	146	1327	172
1967	1520	647	287	206	88	59	32	39	34	62	23	79	1984	287	114	139	2098	271
Total	3488		1048		842		441		343		166		6328		710		7038	
Women:																		
1962	659	–	204	–	1118	–	426	–	173	–	714	–	3294	–	468	–	3762	–
1963	2803	100	1186	100	2011	100	773	100	455	100	1881	100	9109	100	1407	100	10516	100
1964	3571	127	2021	170	1842	92	920	119	600	132	2057	109	11011	121	1670	119	12681	121
1965	5202	186	2644	223	1137	57	753	97	492	108	1914	102	12142	133	1823	140	13965	133
1966	4887	174	2944	248	647	32	493	64	255	56	1322	70	10548	116	1561	111	12109	115
1967	5387	192	4555	484	531	26	403	52	222	49	618	33	11716	129	1500	107	13216	126
Total	22509		13554		7286		3768		2197		8506		57820		8429		66249	
Children:																		
1962	860	–	289	–	1365	–	697	–	248	–	157	–	3616	–	607	–	4223	–
1963	3578	100	1979	100	3361	100	1518	100	553	100	282	100	11371	100	1799	100	13170	100
1964	4870	136	4784	241·7	5805	173	2556	168	1043	189	396	140	19454	171	2417	134	21871	166
1965	7094	198	3915	197·8	6127	182	2785	183	545	99	502	178	20968	184	2876	160	23844	181
1966	7614	213	6210	313·8	2771	176	2771	182	293	53	536	190	23268	205	2426	135	25694	195
1967	8915	249	12664	640	7253	219	2904	191	249	45	462	164	32247	285	2322	129	34769	264
Total	32931		29841		29815		13231		2931		2335		111124		12447		123571	

Source Commonwealth Immigrants Acts Statistics, 1962-7.

We have observed that the proportion of immigrants in the six conurbations has changed during the inter-censal period 1961-6. Thus, the proportion of immigrants from Cyprus and West Africa resident in the six conurbations has increased by 6·3 per cent, while:

India	decreased by	0·4%
Pakistan	,, ,,	8·4%
Jamaica	,, ,,	10·8%
Rest of Caribbean	,, ,,	7·9%

It is possible that these differences have occurred because of changes in the boundary definitions during the period between the two censuses, or because there has been some genuine dispersal of the immigrant population into other urban areas.

(c) *The Commonwealth Immigrants Acts Statistics*
The Commonwealth Immigrants Act statistics are published for each Commonwealth country for five and a half years from July 1962 to December 1967. We have classified approximately thirty territories into seven groups of countries so that each group is comparable to those in the censuses. The seven groups are: India, Pakistan, Jamaica, the rest of the Caribbean, Cyprus, West Africa and the rest of the Commonwealth. We divided the 5½ years into two periods: 3¾ years from July 1962 to April 1966, so as to coincide with the 1966 census date, and a 1¾ year period beginning from the 1966 census date to the end of 1967. This division enables us to observe the changes in the number of immigrants over the entire period, which reflects not only the results of official policy, but also the degree of family reunion already achieved, though it does *not* enable us to extrapolate a trend.

(d) *The Notting Hill Housing Survey*
This is a fully enumerated survey for the entire population of the Notting Hill area. The main tables are presently being analysed by the Social Research Unit at the University of Sussex, but are not as yet available for comment. The eight special tables on demographic data were used extensively in our research; the extent of this survey and its quality provide us for the first time with data which enable us to probe deeply into the family history of the coloured immigrant population. A monograph to be published in 1969 will discuss in detail the results of this survey.

As with the 1966 special tabulations, we designed with the same format tables from the Notting Hill Housing Survey, in which over 5,000 households had been interviewed, of which nearly 1,400 were found to contain coloured immigrants. (See Table 8).

With the exception of Pakistani households, the number of households interviewed from the remaining countries seem adequate for statistical analysis.

Table 8. Country of Origin of Coloured Immigrant Households in the Notting Hill
Survey

Country of Origin	No. of Households
India	78
Pakistan	19
Jamaica	185
Rest of Caribbean	722
West Africa	212
Cyprus	40
East Africa	44
Rest of Commonwealth	66
Non-Commonwealth	24

Source Notting Hill Housing Survey.

Analysis of the Commonwealth Immigrants Acts Statistics

We assume that all persons admitted under the Act in the five categories — long-term
visitors, students, holders of vouchers, dependants and others for settlement — are
potential immigrants. In 1962 they numbered 30,979, but had increased to 69,121
by 1967. Of this number, in the last year, 72 per cent were dependants, 14 per cent
students, 6·9 per cent holders of vouchers, 4·2 per cent other persons for settlement
and 2·8 per cent long-term visitors (see Table 9).

Table 9. Arrival of 'Potential Coloured Commonwealth Immigrants', 1962-7

	Long-Term Visitors		Students		Holders of Vouchers		Dependants		Others for Settlement		Total Persons	
Year	No.	%	No.	%	No.	%	No.	%	No.	%	No.	%
1962	3333	10·2	11201	35·2	4217	13·3	8220	25·9	4008	12·6	30979	100
1963	6575	8·3	16370	20·7	28678	36·3	22459	30·9	2934	3·1	77016	100
1964	5192	6·7	18044	23·4	14837	19·3	35728	46·4	3214	4·2	77015	100
1965	2973	4·7	12382	18·2	12125	16·6	39228	57·6	2297	3·4	69005	100
1966	2315	3·8	12407	20·2	5141	8·4	39130	63·8	2331	3·8	61324	100
1967	1928	2·8	9545	14·0	4716	6·9	50083	72·0	2849	4·2	69121	100
Total	22316	–	79949	–	69714	–	194848	–	17633	–	384460	100

Source Commonwealth Immigrants Acts Statistics, 1962-7.

Taking 1963 as an index of 100, in 1967 each of the five categories is represented as
follows:

Table 10. Index of Categories of 'Potential Coloured Commonwealth Immigrants'
arriving between 1963 and 1967: 1963 = 100

	1963	1964	1965	1966	1967
Dependants	100	159	175	174	223
For Settlement	100	110	78	79	97
Students	100	110	76	78	58
Long-Term Visitors	100	70	45	35	29
Holders of Vouchers	100	52	42	18	16

See Figure 2 below.
Source Commonwealth Immigrants Acts statistics, 1962-7.

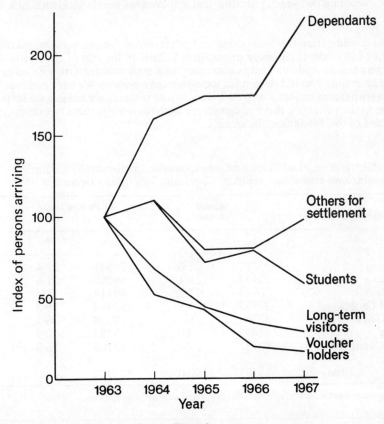

Figure 2.
Arrival of Potential Immigrants 1963-7: Index 1963=100.

During the last two years, the decline in the number of immigrants in all categories except that of dependants is perhaps a reflection of increasing rigour in the implementation of the immigration laws.

From this flow of 385,000 potential permanent immigrants, we determined those persons who are likely to remain, taking into account immigration regulations and social factors. We used the following assumptions for the main categories. A proportion of long-term visitors is likely to remain, but if we were wrong about this, our total estimates would still vary by less than 2 per cent.

Gish points out* that from the white Commonwealth countries in 1966 (here, Australia, Canada and New Zealand), 19,232 or 89 per cent came as long-term visitors (over three months). They are allowed to work without a voucher for a period not exceeding two years, providing that employment is only incidental to a holiday.

Taking into consideration the 'brain drain' and other related factors, we assumed that 25 per cent of all students are likely to remain in Britain. In the case of the West Indians where female students vastly outnumber their male counterparts, we assume that the great majority would remain for socio-economic reasons. We have evidence that the overwhelming majority of West Indian female students are nursing students. All persons in the remaining three categories are likely to remain; these represent 83·5 per cent of the 385,000 actual arrivals.

Table 11. Distribution of all Coloured Commonwealth Immigrants by Countries who have arrived and are likely to remain: July 1962 - December 1967

Country	Actual Arrivals		Persons likely to remain	
	No.	%	No.	%
India	96310	25·0	88041	27·4
Pakistan	73474	19·1	69055	21·4
Jamaica	50924	13·2	49414	15·4
Rest of Caribbean	37553	9·8	32864	10·3
West Africa	32767	8·5	19628	6·1
Cyprus	11445	3·0	9253	2·9
Other Commonwealth	82722	21·4	53105	16·5
Total	385195	100·0	321360	100·0

Source Commonwealth Immigrants Acts Statistics and authors' calculations.

* Oscar Gish, 'Alien, Old Commonwealth and New Commonwealth Workers', *Race,* Vol. IX, No. 4 (April 1968).

Table 12.   Arrival of Total Persons, Males, Females and Children from all Commonwealth Countries in three Periods, who are likely to remain: July 1962 —
December 1967

	Total Persons	Males	Females	Children
July 1962 - April 1966	222162	72758	73154	76250
August 1966 - December 1967	99208	14944	28644	55620
July 1962 - December 1967	321360	87692	101798	131870

Source   Home Office statistics of arrivals and authors' calculations.

The ratio of men, women and children in the first period was 7 : 7 : 8, but in the
latter it was 15 : 29 : 56, or twice as many women as men, and four times as many
children as men.

There is an uneven distribution of persons likely to remain among the different
countries, which is more pronounced in the last one and three-quarter years in this
period. India alone accounts for 6,830 (46·0 per cent) of 14,944 adult male immigrants;
this is followed by Pakistan with 2,405 persons. As we shall see later, most of these
are voucher holders. During the latter period, most of the children arriving in Britain
were Pakistanis, and account for one-third of all new arrivals.

As the category of dependants accounts for three out of four immigrants, we intend
to examine in greater detail the dynamic changes which have occurred during the
period following the Act. The number of dependent persons increased from 8,220
persons in 1962 to 50,083 in 1966, which amounts in total to 196,858 persons.
They include 7,038 men, 66,249 women and 123,371 children (see Figure 3). The
following table gives a breakdown for all Commonwealth countries. (The details for
each country are given in Table 7).

Table 13.   Arrival of Total Coloured Commonwealth Dependent Persons for 5½ Years:
July 1962 - December 1967

	Total Persons	Men	Women	Children	Index Increase (1963=100)
India	60127	3488	22509	32931	239
Pakistan	44443	1048	13554	29841	530
Jamaica	37943	842	7286	29815	141
Rest of Caribbean	17380	441	3768	13231	141
Cyprus	5471	343	2197	2931	48
West Africa	11107	166	8506	2335	79
Rest of Commonwealth	21586	710	8429	12447	120
Total	196858	7038	66249	123371	

Source   Commonwealth Immigrants Acts Statistics, 1962-7.

Except for Indians since 1965, the proportion of dependent men to the total of dependent persons, has been declining rapidly, to negligible numbers. We cannot account for the 1,520 Indian male adult dependants who arrived in 1967, which we consider to be extraordinary. Presumably some of them were fathers of immigrants and were of pensionable age.

Arrivals of women dependants from all countries, except India and Pakistan, have declined by as much as 25-50 per cent during the period 1963-6. This is more noticeable in the case of Jamaica. Pakistani women, on the other hand, have consistently increased in numbers to the extent that in 1967 twice as many arrived as in 1966. However, in relation to all dependants, the proportion of women dependants has nearly halved for most countries during the five-year period.

Table 14. Index of the Arrival of Women Dependants from Coloured Commonwealth Countries in 1967 compared to 1963

	% (1963 = 100)	No. in 1967
India	192	(5387)
Pakistan	484	(4555)
Jamaica	26	(531)
Rest of Caribbean	52	(403)
Cyprus	49	(222)
West Africa	33	(618)
Rest of Commonwealth	107	(1500)

Source Commonwealth Immigrants Acts Statistics and authors' calculations.

Dependent children of immigrants from all countries increased from 4,223 in 1963 to 34,709 in 1967. Only Cyprus, since 1965, has shown a steady decrease. There has been a very considerable increase of Pakistani children during this period. In 1967 there were over 12,000 children, from the country, who alone accounted for 33 per cent of all children from coloured Commonwealth countries. There have also been substantial increases from India and the West Indies (see Table 15).

Table 15. Dependent Children in 1967 as an Index of those in 1963: 1963 = 100

	Index	No. in 1967
India	249	8915
Pakistan	640	12664
Jamaica	219	7253
Rest of Caribbean	191	2904
Cyprus	45	249
West Africa	164	462
Rest of Commonwealth	129	2322

Source Commonwealth Immigrants Acts Statistics and authors' calculations.

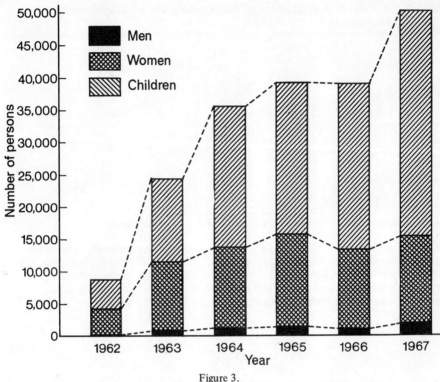

Figure 3.
Arrival of Dependants (Men, Women and Children) 1962-7.

The majority of the dependants of immigrants are now arriving from India and
Pakistan. In 1967, these two countries accounted for 68 per cent of all immigrant
dependants (see Table 16).

There were four distinct stages in the building up of the coloured immigrant
population from Commonwealth countries in Great Britain. The first stage of slow
growth lasted until 1951, when there were approximately only 100,000 persons. In
the second stage from 1951 to 1960, the gradual building up process began, so that
by the end of this period the coloured population increased by nearly three times.
Then between 1960 until the passing of the Commonwealth Immigrants Act in 1962,
there was accelerated growth which accounted for one out of every three immigrants
in 1966. This sudden influx consisted only of immigrants from a few countries. The
net inward flow of immigrants from Pakistan to the United Kingdom increased in
one year from 1960 to 1961 from a low level of 2,500 by ten times to 25,000
persons, and from India, the increase was four times the 1960 total of nearly 6,000
persons. But the largest number came from the West Indies, which accounted for

Table 16. Arrivals of Dependants from each Country 1962-7 as a Percentage of all Dependants

Year	India	Pakistan	Jamaica	Rest of Caribbean	Cyprus	West Africa	Rest of the Commonwealth	Total
1962	19	6	31	14	5	11	14	100
1963	27	14	23	11	4	9	12	100
1964	25	20	22	10	5	7	11	100
1965	33	17	19	9	3	6	13	100
1966	35	24	17	8	2	5	6	100
1967	32	36	16	7	1	2	6	100

Source Commonwealth Immigrants Acts Statistics and authors' calculations.

66,000 immigrants in 1961 or 50 per cent of coloured Commonwealth immigrants from all countries. The fourth stage is from mid-1962 to the present time. In it, there is the consolidation of immigrant households which is based on the arrivals of dependants who are mostly wives and children. Let us now examine the main characteristics of the immigrant population in the post-1962 period.

Chapter 3 / The Coloured Commonwealth Immigrant Population in 1966

Under-enumerated Immigrants

In order to assess the validity of the 1966 Census, it is necessary to determine the degree of its under-enumeration. This can be ascertained by net arrivals, that is the difference between all arrivals and all departures. The Institute's 'Survey of Race Relations' in Britain has used this method. (See Table 17: note that the calculations for Indians and Pakistanis exclude the white element.) The reliability of this method, although theoretically good, is based on estimates for a period of fifteen years which in our opinion may be inadequate to test the authenticity of the departure section of the calculations.

Since the annual statistics of the Commonwealth Immigrants Acts show greater detail for men, women and children and provide a breakdown of all categories of arrivals, we can with a great deal of accuracy determine those arrivals who are most likely to remain as immigrants. We include here all dependants, persons for settlement, voucher holders and a small proportion of students and long-term visitors. The total of

Table 17. Survey of Race Relations in Britain: Adjustment of Census Estimates by Reference to Net Arrivals

	India*	Pakistan*	Jamaica	Rest of the Caribbean	West Africa	East Africa	Cyprus and Malta	Ceylon	Hong Kong, Malaysia
Census 1951									
	30800	5000	6400	8900	5600	3900	24700	5800	12000
Net Arrivals, Jan. '55 to Census '61									
	37900	22100	106200	71300	7900	3400			
Joint Estimate									
	68700	27100	112600	80200	13500	7300			
Census 1961									
	81400	24900	100100	71700	19800	10600	66600	9000	29900
Best Estimates '61									
	81400	27100	112600	80200	19800	10600	66600	9000	29900
Net Arrivals, Census '61 to Census '66									
	99000	82500	75500	49600	23300	11400	21600	3400	6500
Joint Estimate									
	180400	109600	188100	129800	43100	22000	88200	12400	36400
Census 1966									
	158200	68500	151800	116000	36000	31300	90800	12900	47000
Best Estimate 1966									
	180400	109600	188100	129800	43100	31300	90800	12900	47000
Estimated Census Under-enumeration in 1966 (minimum)									
	22000	41100	36300	13800	7100	–	–	–	–

Total Under-enumeration   120300

* Excluding whites.
Source Survey of Race Relations in Britain.

persons in Table 18 and following is determined for three and three-quarter years which is from the beginning of the Act of July 1962 to the 1966 Census.

To complete the five-year intercensal period, for the period 1961-2, we took estimates as provided by the General Register Office. In addition to the three and three-quarter years of the Commonwealth Immigrants Act statistics, we obtained the five-year inward flow. We next determined the outward flow and again used the General Register Office's estimates. These were given in two aggregates for India, Pakistan and Ceylon and the West Indies. We found the mean for the period and then divided the numbers for the West Indies, that is, 75 per cent for Jamaica and 25 per cent for the rest of the West Indies, according to the composition of the migrants from these countries in the 1961 Census. A similar method with some modifications was used for the three Asian countries. Having found the total reflux we subtracted this number from the five-year growth estimate and thus obtained the estimated net

Table 18. Under-enumeration in the 1966 Census of Coloured Commonwealth
Population in England and Wales

	India	Pakistan	Jamaica	Rest of Caribbean
	No.	No.	No.	No.
Estimate of arrivals after 1961 Census to the Act − 1¼ years	40000	43905	46587	34938
Arrivals from the Act to the 1966 Census − 3¾ years	56004	42103	35110	35110
Total increase 5 years	96866	86008	81697	70048
Reflux 5 years	11000	13000	12600	9400
Net arrivals calculated	85866	73008	69097	60648
1966 Census	232210	73130	151840	116800
1961 Census	157435	30737	100051	72328
Five Year Growth	74775	42393	51781	44472
Difference between 5-year net arrivals and calculated 5-year census growth	11091	30615	17316	16176
Best estimate of population; 1966 Census: gross	243301	103745	169156	132976
minus white Indians	68600			
Best estimate of population: net	174701	98745	169156	132976
% under-enumeration by our estimate	4·6	29·5	10·2	12·2

Source Commonwealth Immigrants Acts Statistics and authors' calculations.

arrivals. There are no means available in this short period to test the accuracy of the
General Register Office's estimates which we have apportioned to each country. Even
our distribution method may be questioned.

The next step is to ascertain the difference between the 1961 and 1966 Censuses.
Since the numbers of the white section of the Indian and Pakistan population in
Britain has decreased without any certain explanation we have retained their numbers
in the total population for the two censuses. We have assumed that their mortality
rate would have the same pattern as that of the British, though they would in all
probability be somewhat older than the home population.

Finally, we obtained the actual number who were under-enumerated as the difference
between the five-year census growth and the estimated arrivals in the same period.
The percentage of under-enumeration is: India 4·6 per cent; Pakistan 29·5 per cent;
Jamaica 10·2 per cent; rest of the Caribbean 12·2 per cent (see Table 18). Our
estimate of the under-enumeration of the total coloured population for the four
groups of countries is 75,200 as compared to the 120,300 estimate of the Survey of
Race Relations in Britain.

The Significance of the under-enumerated Population

The importance of the under-enumerated population depends upon the marital status of all persons. It is most likely that these are adult males who are either single, or do not have their wives in this country; if this is so, then a large proportion of dependants would be expected to arrive. But they could also be more evenly spread, with a high proportion of children under-enumerated.

We have to take cognizance of the under-enumerated population in the final estimate of dependants who are likely to arrive. Since the probability is that such immigrants have more dependants than others in their country of origin, allowance has been made for a greater increase from this source (see p. 48).

The total number of under-enumerated Indians is nearly 11,000 persons, but represents only 4·6 per cent in this ethnic group. The large number of Pakistanis is probably comprised of males who are married without any member of their family in the host country. The upward trend in the arrivals of dependent Pakistani females and children may be partly ascribed to this significant proportion of under-enumerated persons and the large number enumerated as married, but without any member of their family in this country.

Persons in Coloured Commonwealth Immigrant Households born in England and Wales

By comparing the two tables of the 1966 Census special tabulations (relating especially to the London and Midlands areas), we are able to determine the birthplace of children and adults, the marital status of adults, and the number of males who are married but without their wives. This is done by subtracting Table 1 from Table 2 of these special tabulations; in other words, by subtracting persons in households where the head of household is born in a specified country (A), from persons in households which may comprise more than one nationality (A+X), where X = persons of a different nationality. For example, in Indian households there were 85,830 persons, while 56,886 persons were actually born in India. Hence 28,944 persons born outside India were living in Indian households.

Immigrants who are without their Wives, or are separated from their Wives

From the birthplace table we know the number of married men from each country, while the household table indicates the number of married women. Therefore the difference between these two tables shows the number of married men who are without their wives (see Table 19). This Table indicates that only 25 per cent of Pakistani married men have their wives in England. 6,791 of the 10,523 wives arrived during the first three and three-quarter years of the Commonwealth Immigrants Act. A further 6,763 wives arrived after the 1966 Census, so that by the end of 1967, 24,600 married Pakistanis were still without their wives. From other countries, however, only a very small proportion of married men were without their wives by the end of 1967.

Table 19.   Married Men with their Wives in the Country of Origin who are expected
to arrive from January 1968.

	Married men with wives abroad	No. of married women in household	Total no. of married men (Col. 1+ Col. 2)	No. of women dependants who arrived from 1966 census to Dec. 1967	Married women expected to arrive from Jan. 1968 (Col. 4 − Col. 1)	Percentage expected to arrive to married males	
						1966 census (Col. 5 ÷ Col. 1)	Notting Hill Survey
	Col. 1	Col. 2	Col. 3	Col. 4	Col. 5	Col. 6	Col. 7
	No.	No.	No.	No.	No.	%	%
India	14000	62137	76039	9052	4948	6·5	15·8
Pakistan	31300	10523	41819	6763	24637	59·0	8·6
Jamaica	3600	47965	51582	1016	2584	5·0	6·5
Rest of Caribbean	1100	33304	34951	773	327	0·9	8·4
Cyprus	−	20064	19959	413	−	−	−
West Africa	3500	11326	14846	1610	1890	12·7	11·0

Source   Special Tabulations; Notting Hill Housing Survey and authors' calculations.

Inter-marriage

If we assume that all married immigrant women are in households with married men
of the same country of origin, then the difference between the two tables — persons
in households, and country of origin — gives us the number of women who are in
households where the head of the household was born in a different country of
origin. Table 20 shows that a significant proportion of these women are in the 15-19
and 20-24 year age groups. The proportion in 1966 differs from the 1961 Census but
is consistent with the Notting Hill Survey. The apparent increased proportion in the
younger age groups is an indication of the greater frequency of mixed marriages.
The Notting Hill Survey shows that, except for the Indians, a very insignificant
proportion of coloured women have married males from countries other than their
own. The majority of inter-marriages are with white citizens of the United Kingdom.
(see Table 21).

From the Notting Hill Survey we know that among all heads of households whose
conjugal status was married, living without a spouse, widowed, separated and divorced,
64·6 per cent had a spouse who was from the same country of origin; 9·6 per cent of
males had wives born elsewhere (5·9 per cent were from Great Britain); 19·0 per cent
were husbands or wives living alone; and 9·5 per cent were widowed, separated and
divorced. The most striking feature of this table of the Survey is that only 6·3 per cent
of males have their wives abroad. As we have seen, this proportion does not differ
significantly from the 1966 Census special tabulations.

Another important finding from the Notting Hill Survey is that there is hardly any
inter-marriage with nationals in the immediate geographic region of the country of
origin of immigrants — Indians, Pakistanis and Singhalese have not inter-married.

Table 20. Age Structure of Females in Households who were not born in the Country of Origin of the Male

	No. of married men	Per cent inter-marriage among males	Total females in households not of the country of origin of head	Age Group of Females 15-19	Age Group of Females 20-24	Age Group of Females 25-44	Age Group of Females 45 & over	Notting Hill Survey	Notting Hill Survey	Notting Hill Survey
	No.		No.	No.	No.	No.	No.	No.	No.	%
India	76039	7·5	5731	164	1041	4526	–	6	(32)*	19
Pakistan	41819	6·2	2571	100	730	1564	177	4	(7)	45
Jamaica	51582	3·3	1683	83	468	965	166	19	(100)	19
Rest of Caribbean	34957	5·1	1787	57	447	1283	–	31	(414)	8
Cyprus	19959	18·1	3613	140	662	2049	762	6	(26)	23
West Africa	14846	6·5	961	58	44	758	101	12	(135)	9

* Total respondents.

Source Special Tabulations, Notting Hill Housing Survey and authors' calculations.

Table 21. Coloured Commonwealth Immigrant Households with Mixed Marriages, 1961 Census (per cent of Total Households)

	Total households		Head and spouse born in country of origin		Head U.K.–spouse country of origin		Head U.K.–spouse country of origin		All others	
	No.	%	No.	%	No.	%	No.	%	No.	%
India	26526	100	7384	28	7787	28	5864	22	5491	22
Pakistan	3323	100	818	25	1182	36	315	11	1008	29
Jamaica	14002	100	9381	67	1400	10	238	2	2983	11
Rest of Caribbean	10235	100	5477	54	1366	13·4	359	4	3033	19

Source 1961 Census of England and Wales Commonwealth Immigrants in the Conurbations, Table B5 and authors' calculations.

To a lesser extent this is evident in the case of Jamaicans and other Commonwealth Caribbean countries. Even in their households we have found very few cases where there are members who are not from the same country of origin as the head of the household.

The 1961 Census, however, shows that among Indians and Pakistanis there were many households where the wife was not born in the same country as the head of the household. This is because of the larger proportion of white heads of household who were born in India or Pakistan. For Jamaica and the rest of the Caribbean the reverse is the case. But where mixed marriages do take place it is usually with citizens from Great Britain (see Table 21). In comparison to 1966 (see Table 20), the number of inter-marriages has not increased significantly, whereas the proportion against all married men has declined immensely.

Marital Status

We have observed that for nearly all the countries there is a very large proportion of single males and females over the age of 20 years, as shown in these pyramids.

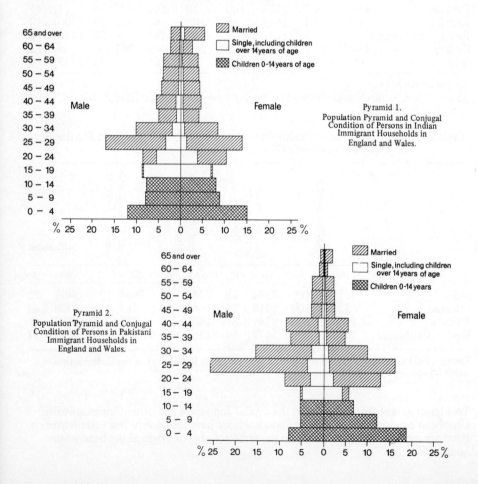

Pyramid 1.
Population Pyramid and Conjugal Condition of Persons in Indian Immigrant Households in England and Wales.

Pyramid 2.
Population Pyramid and Conjugal Condition of Persons in Pakistani Immigrant Households in England and Wales.

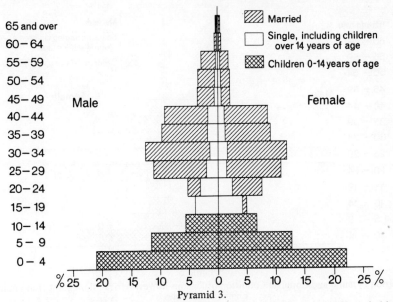

Pyramid 3.
Population Pyramid and Conjugal Condition of Persons in Jamaican Immigrant Households in England and Wales.

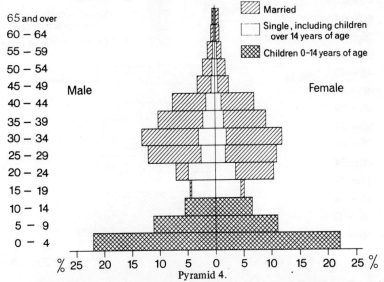

Pyramid 4.
Population Pyramid and Conjugal Condition of Persons in Rest of the Caribbean Countries' Immigrant Households in England and Wales.

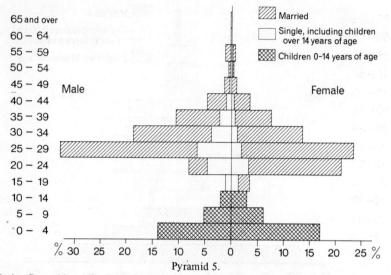

Pyramid 5.
Population Pyramid and Conjugal Condition of Persons in West African Immigrant Households in England and Wales.

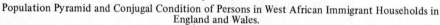

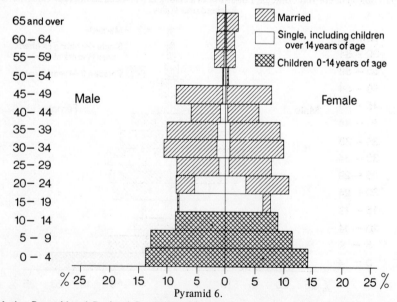

Pyramid 6.
Population Pyramid and Conjugal Condition of Persons in Cypriot Immigrant Households in England and Wales.

Among no immigrant group does there appear to be a shortage of males or females eligible for marital union from the same country of origin. There are 14,000 single Indian males of 25-44 years, against 4,500 single females. Among the Jamaicans there are only 2,000 fewer single females than single males (Table 22). Only among the Pakistanis are there far more single males than females.

According to the United Nations *Demographic Yearbook 1965** the number of single Indian males is 28 million out of a total population of 134 million males over 15 years of age. If we assume that all 15-19 year old males are single and that they are part of the 28 million single males, this leaves only 9 million males who are 19 years and over and single. They would represent 7·7 per cent of the total adult male population over 19 years of age. If we apply the same method of deducting the 15-19 year age group from the total single males and females for Pakistan and females for India, there would be no single females or males in the total population over 19 years of age. This is an indication that, except for Indian males, only a very small proportion of the total adult population remain single in their country of origin after the age of 19.

It is possible to account for the extensive single status of West Indians by the practice of the system of consensual unions; but even so we have no evidence of its large-scale practice in this country. The Notting Hill Survey shows that only a rather insignificant number of single women have children. And in their household composition, there is no convincing evidence of the practice of the system on a large-scale (that is, there are few single adult males and females in the same household).

For the remaining Commonwealth countries, we do not know of a national system of family life that would enable us to account for this phenomenon. Again, we find evidence that there is a large proportion of adults who are single in the Notting Hill Survey (see Table 23).

We do know that in their country of origin, the vast majority of all persons between 19 and 44 years have some form of marital relationship. This means that coloured Commonwealth immigrants in Britain have modified their marriage patterns, and that in some respects they are now more similar to those of the British. This should ultimately result in reduced fertility rates among immigrants in Britain.

Among those coloured Commonwealth immigrants who are married, there seems to be a tendency for marriage to take place at a later age than would be normal in the country of origin. Nearly 75 per cent of all immigrant women are aged between 20 and 44 years. Since this is the most fertile period, it would be expected that the birth rate among immigrants is high (see Figure 4). On the other hand, however, among Indians and Pakistanis — whose early marriage is the norm in their countries of origin — less than 1 per cent of females under 19 in this country are married;

---

* United Nations, *Demographic Yearbook 1965* (New York, 1966).

Table 22. Single Males and Females for each of the Six Groups of Countries by Age Group

	India Males	India Females	Pakistan Males	Pakistan Females	Jamaica Males	Jamaica Females	Rest of Caribbean Males	Rest of Caribbean Females	Cyprus Males	Cyprus Females	West Africa Males	West Africa Females
20 - 24	8995	5181	2196	2527	3722	2837	4007	3977	2083	3588	1214	758
25 - 44	14308	4549	5180	556	9427	7064	8492	5635	1832	1165	3865	888
45 - 59	1716	2090	477	126	1536	1405	868	1009	353	3524	135	—
60 - 64	419	566	48	26	44	179	116	159	38	585	—	—
65 +	273	1262	72	50	87	110	14	130	12	814	15	—
Total single	25711	13648	7973	3285	14816	11595	13497	10910	4318	9676	5229	1646
Total married	76000	58000	42000	8000	52000	46000	35000	32000	20000	17000	15000	10000
% of single to married	34	24	19	41	28	25	39	34	22	57	35	16

Source Special Tabulations.

Table 23. Households by Marital Status: Conjugal Conditions of Adults in Households (Notting Hill Survey)

	India No.	India %	Pakistan No.	Pakistan %	Jamaica No.	Jamaica %	Rest of Caribbean No.	Rest of Caribbean %	Commonwealth West Africa No.	Commonwealth West Africa %	Cyprus No.	Cyprus %	Commonwealth East Africa No.	Commonwealth East Africa %	Remainder of Commonwealth No.	Remainder of Commonwealth %	Coloured non-Commonwealth No.	Coloured non-Commonwealth %	Total Households No.	Total Households %
Married (husband and wife)	38	48·7	7	36·8	102	54·6	416	57·6	135	63·3	28	70	19	43·3	41	62·1	12	50	798	57·4
Married without wife	6	7·7	0	—	7	3·8	35	4·5	15	7·0	0	—	1	2·3	2	3·0	—	—	66	4·8
Married without husband	0	—	0	—	8	4·3	70	9·7	7	3·3	2	5	1	2·3	2	3·0	—	—	90	6·5
Single male	21	26·9	11	57·9	21	11·4	90	12·5	44	20·5	4	10	17	36·6	9	13·6	11	45·8	228	16·4
Single female	9	11·5	1	5·3	30	16·2	59	8·2	5	7·3	2	5	3	6·8	9	13·6	—	—	118	8·5
Widowed male	0	—	0	—	1	0·5	3	0·4	0	—	0	—	—	—	1	1·5	—	—	5	0·4
Widowed female	3	3·8	0	—	7	3·8	13	1·8	1	0·5	2	5	2	4·5	2	3·0	—	—	30	2·1
Separated and divorced males	0	—	0	—	2	1·1	13	1·8	4	1·9	0	—	0	—	0	—	—	—	19	1·4
Separated and divorced females	1	1·3	0	—	7	4·3	23	3·2	1	0·5	2	5	1	2·3	—	—	1	4·2	36	2·6
Total	78		19		185		722		212		40		44		66		24		1390	

Source Notting Hill Housing Survey.

this would confirm a trend towards adjustment to British marriage patterns. None-theless, there has been an enormous increase in the number of married persons in the five-year period; this is mostly for the Caribbean countries.

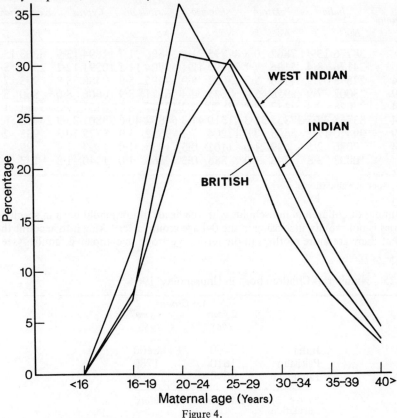

Figure 4.
Live Births according to maternal Age and ethnic Groups in Birmingham 1966.

Age Structure

The age structure of persons in the immigrant population also shows the following peculiarities. For nearly all countries there are as many persons under 4 years of age as in the 45-59 years age group. The population under 19 years of age represents 38 per cent of the total persons in Indian households. This proportion is nearly the same for all countries (see Table 24).

When we compare the 1966 household age structure with the national age structure of the population of immigrants' countries of origin, we see that the age group 0-19 years nearly coincides with their normal age pyramid.

Table 24. Age Structure of Coloured Commonwealth Immigrant Population in Households, 1966: Per cent of Total Population

Age Group	India		Pakistan		Jamaica		Rest of Caribbean		Cyprus		West Africa	
	No.	%	No.	%	No.	%	No.	%	No.	%	No.	%
0 -4	38776	13·4	7862	10·8	47775	21·6	34686	21·7	11894	13·9	6363	15·2
5 - 9	24176	8·4	5186	7·1	26999	12·1	17704	11·1	10391	12·2	2343	5·6
10 - 14	22878	7·9	4148	5·7	13032	5·9	9495	5·9	7488	8·8	993	2·4
15 - 19	23007	7·9	3956	5·4	9645	4·4	6171	3·9	6806	8·0	860	2·1
20 - 24	27028	9·4	7187	9·9	13830	6·3	13787	8·6	8157	9·6	5711	1·4
25 - 44	83765	34·5	37337	51·3	91310	41·3	64832	40·6	28801	33·9	24475	58·5
45 - 59	99410	12·2	5668	7·9	17204	7·7	9552	5·9	8775	10·3	935	2·2
60 - 64	7086	2·5	699	1·0	1161	0·5	1055	1·0	1199	1·4	29	–
65+	10833	3·8	748	1·0	588	0·3	868	1·0	1540	1·8	133	–

Source Special Tabulations.

The number of children in households with the heads of household born in specified countries is not rapidly increasing in the 0-4 age group, after taking into account the fact that there are more mothers in the fertile age group in completed families (see Table 25).

Table 25. Number of Children born in Households: 1964-5

	Age Group	
	2 years 1964	1 year 1965
India	7400	8200
Pakistan	1610	1780
Jamaica	9290	10400

Source Special Tabulations and authors' calculations.

Children of Coloured Commonwealth Immigrants born in England

Most of the children in coloured Commonwealth immigrant households were not born in their parents' country of origin. Except for a few who were born in other countries, the majority were born in the British Isles. We shall therefore consider the birthplace of the children of coloured Commonwealth immigrants who were not born in their parents' country of origin, to be England and Wales. The numbers were obtained from the difference between the household tables (Appendix 2A-F) and the birthplace tables (Appendix 1A-F). The percentage distribution of children in each age group compares favourably with the Notting Hill Survey and the 1966 Census special tabulations. Table 26 shows the proportions for India.

Table 26. Proportion of Children in Indian Households born in England and Wales

Age Groups	Per Cent 1966 Census	Notting Hill Survey
0 - 4	88·6	93·8
5 - 9	60·0	62·5
10 - 14	35·2	40·0
15 - 19	21·1	18·2

Source Special Tabulations and Notting Hill Housing Survey.

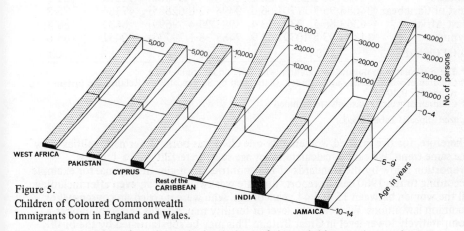

Figure 5.
Children of Coloured Commonwealth
Immigrants born in England and Wales.

The most astonishing fact about the birthplace of these children is that in the 0-4 year age group, 47,775 or 98·1 per cent of children in Jamaican households were born in the United Kingdom. Even in the 5-9 year age group, 80·2 and 60·0 per cent of Jamaican and Indian children respectively were born in this country. More than two out of three children in all immigrant households except for Pakistani were born in England and Wales (see Table 27). These children, who are now citizens of the United Kingdom as are their white counterparts, numbered 210,000 in 1966. For our groupings of six coloured Commonwealth countries, plus all the remaining countries, the total would be 263,000 children.

Fertility

Although the number of married Indian females increased by 11,000 during the period 1961-6, nearly 50 per cent (or 19,000) of all Indian children in the 0-4 age group were born in Britain. Therefore this large net increase of married women has not substantially reduced the number of Indian children, whose place of birth is not in the host country, during the five-year period. We have also observed that there were 46.000 married females in Indian households in 1966 between 19-44 years of age. The total number of children born to these women were 8,200 in 1965 and 8,500 in 1966.

Table 27. Children in Coloured Commonwealth Households born in England and
Wales* as a Proportion of all Children in Households

	Children in Households and percentage of those born in England and Wales						Children 0-14 years of age born in England and Wales	
	0-4		5-9		10-14		Total	Proportion to all Children in Households	
	No.	%	No.	%	No.	%	No.	No.	%
India**	38776	88·6	24176	60·0	22878	35·2	85830	56886	66·3
Pakistan†	7863	73·3	5186	32·5	4148	0·1	17197	7427	43·2
Jamaica	47775	98·1	26999	80·2	13032	20·7	87806	71218	81·1
Rest of Caribbean	34686	96·7	17704	66·0	9495	12·0	62885	47364	75·3
West Africa	6363	86·5	2343	33·4	993	25·4	9699	6632	68·4
Cyprus	11894	93·5	10391	62·9	7488	38·1	29773	20431	68·6
Total Children		100		100		100			100

* These estimates do not include children who were under-enumerated.
** Children of white Indians are included. (Estimated by Survey of Race Relations in Britain
 to number 9,000.)
† Children of white Pakistanis are included.

Source Special Tabulations.

Therefore, for five married women only one child was born. Other nationalities show
the same trend. We cannot calculate exact age-specific fertility rates, but this
proportion is low by the standards of the countries of origin. In Guyana, for example,
according to the 1960 census report, this rate was twice as great, even after including
all the women between 15 and 44 years of age, who were married, in consensual or
common law unions. Whatever the level of fertility may be, this certainly implies a
comparatively lower level in Great Britain. This may be substantiated by the birth
rate in the Birmingham County Borough area. In 1963 there were 2,768 live births
to Jamaican parents, but despite the increase of women in the fertile age group, this
peak dropped by 19·9 per cent reaching 2,188 in 1966.

The number of dependent children by five-year age groups is divided into size of
households with children. According to the 1966 Census, we know that of 76,800
Indian households, 49·6 per cent have no children. In the case of the Pakistanis, the
proportion is 58·8 per cent; for the Jamaicans 35·2 per cent; the rest of the
Caribbean 37·7 per cent; West Africa 69·1 per cent, and for Cyprus 36·5 per cent (see
Table 28). In the case of Indian and Pakistani immigrants this proportion has not
changed since 1961. Table 28 also shows that for most countries in our original
group, there are slightly more than two children to all households with children, but
less than two children for each married woman in the households.

Another important feature of household composition is the age distribution of
children. For most nationalities which have one and two child households, about
half have children who are over four years of age. If family planning were not
practised extensively there would not have been so many children of over five years

Table 28. Distribution of Children by Size of Households, and average Size of Households

	India		Pakistan		Jamaica		Rest of Caribbean		West Africa		Cyprus	
	No.	%	No.	%	No.	%	No.	%	No.	%	No.	%
Number of dependent children in household: 1	12855	33·2	2629	35·2	10723	31·5	8845	32·7	2786	54·7	4700	31·5
2	11854	30·6	2219	29·7	9981	29·3	8454	31·3	1125	22·1	5266	29·3
3	7086	18·3	1351	18·1	6999	20·6	4725	17·5	608	11·9	2841	20·6
4	3682	9·5	722	10·3	4143	12·2	2876	10·6	311	6·1	1124	12·2
5 or more	3212	8·3	506	6·8	2184	6·4	2124	7·9	266	5·2	581	6·4
Households with children	38689		7477		34030		27024		5096		14512	
Total households	76808		19898		54887		43370		16480		21389	
Households without children	38118		12422		19318		16346		11382		7351	
Per cent of households without children to all households		49·6		58·8		35·2		37·7		69·1		36·5
Number of children in all households	90854		17241		88875		63401		9515		31490	
Average number of children to all households with children	2·35		2·30		2·61		2·35		1·87		2·17	
Average number of children to all married women in households	1·46		1·64		1·85		1·90		1·57		1·57	

Source Special Tabulations.

of age in such households. Indeed, as many as one-third of all the children who are between 10 and 14 years of age are in the one and two child households (see Table 29). In most less developed countries, with a high birth rate, children in this age group would be in three or four child households. This is a further indication that immigrants are restricting their family size, which is already different in many respects to that in their country of origin.

Table 29. Per cent Distribution of Children 10-14 years of age by Size of Households with Dependant Children

	India	Pakistan	Jamaica	Rest of Caribbean	West Africa	Cyprus
	%	%	%	%	%	%
No. of Dependent children:						
1	14·2	12·9	13·7	12·6	13·6	12·9
2	22·1	23·1	22·0	19·6	10·2	30·4
3	24·1	23·1	19·3	17·1	22·0	28·3
4	18·9	15·6	17·3	22·0	30·5	16·7
5 or more	20·7	25·3	27·7	28·9	23·7	11·6
No. of children in this age group	22878	4148	13032	9495	993	7488

Source Special Tabulations.

From the Notting Hill Survey, our estimate of complete nuclear families in this country shows that the average size of families is consistent with the data given above. There is also evidence that more children in the one and two child households are over five years of age. This is more pronounced for the West Indians than for the Asians.

There is, however, a very large proportion of children who are under four years of age. Indeed, they account for nearly half of all the children in coloured immigrant households (see Table 30). The most important reason which is responsible for this situation is the arrival of large numbers of married women who are completing their families in this country. Although this is an inevitable process, we are convinced from our analysis of the existing data that it should not result in the larger family sizes which exist in the less developed countries.

In an analysis of the future arrival of dependants, we have to take into account the number of persons born in this country and those who were under-enumerated in the 1966 census. Furthermore, we have to consider the implications of completed family profiles of immigrants as indicated by their marital status, age structure of adults and children and the average size of households.

Table 30. Age Distribution of Children in Households as a Percentage of all Children.

Age of child	India	Pakistan	Jamaica	Rest of Caribbean	Africa	Cyprus
Under 1	9·3	9·8	10·6	10·9	23·6	7·6
Age 1	9·0	10·4	10·5	11·5	17·8	7·6
,, 2	8·2	9·4	11·8	11·4	9·1	6·6
,, 3	8·3	7·4	11·0	10·9	8·4	9·0
,, 4	7·7	7·7	9·4	9·4	6·7	8·0
Total 0-4	42·4	44·7	53·3	54·1	65·6	38·8
Age 5	5·6	6·6	7·1	7·3	7·3	6·8
,, 6	6·0	6·5	6·8	6·2	4·8	7·8
,, 7	4·9	6·2	6·2	5·4	4·2	6·4
,, 8	4·8	5·8	5·1	5·2	3·9	6·0
,, 9	5·1	4·9	4·5	3·5	3·8	6·8
Total 5-9	26·4	30·0	29·7	27·6	24·0	33·8
Age 10	4·7	4·6	3·3	3·2	1·8	5·5
,, 11	5·3	4·1	2·7	3·5	2·5	5·9
,, 12	4·7	4·2	2·9	2·5	2·0	4·5
,, 13	4·7	4·2	2·7	2·7	1·7	3·6
,, 14	4·7	3·5	2·8	2·6	1·2	4·1
Total 10-14	24·0	20·6	14·4	14·5	9·2	23·6
Age 15	2·5	2·4	1·2	1·5	0·3	2·3
,, 16	2·1	0·7	0·9	1·1	0·2	1·4
,, 17	0·9	0·9	0·3	0·5	0·2	0·1
,, 18	0·4	0·4	0·2	0·3	–	–
,, 19	0·5	0·1	–	0·2	0·2	–
,, 20	0·6	0·2	–	0·2	0·3	–
Total 15-20	7·0	4·7	2·6	3·8	1·2	3·8

Source Special Tabulations.

Chapter 4 / Estimates of Future Dependants According to the Commonwealth Immigrants Acts

The method of family profile analysis enables us to estimate the number of dependants – men, women and children – who ought to have arrived since the enactment of the Commonwealth Immigrants Act of 1962. That is to say, taking into account the immigrants who were enumerated in 1961 and are known to have arrived since, we have tried to estimate how many dependants ought to have followed them to complete 'normal' family structures. For the period between the 1961 Census and 1 July 1962, when the Commonwealth Immigrants Act came into force, we do not have a detailed breakdown of the status of new arrivals. Therefore in the main, our calculations are based on the statistics under the Act, though we have corrected these in the light of the 1966 census. We should make it clear, however, that when we speak of the arrival of dependants after mid-1962, we relate them to all immigrants already in the United Kingdom whether they arrived before 1961, in the period 1961 to July 1962, or since that time.

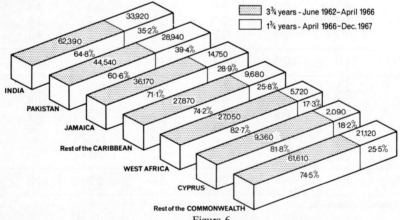

Figure 6.

Actual Arrival of Dependants in 5½ years in two Periods: June 1962-April 1966 (3¾ years) and April 1966-December 1967 (1¾ years).

These dependants were calculated, not on actual arrivals, but on that proportion of arrivals which we have defined as persons likely to remain. We based our assumption on empirical evidence from studies of immigrant populations in their countries of origin and on studies done in this country. By using the assumptions already discussed (see page 2) we have estimated that 84 per cent of 385,190 actual arrivals in the five main categories of 'potential' immigrants are likely to remain. Table 31 shows the difference between actual arrivals and persons likely to remain. Appendix 2 contains detailed calculations for each country and for each category.

Table 31. Arrival of 'Potential Coloured Commonwealth Immigrants', 1962-7

	Actual Arrivals				Persons likely to remain			
	Total	Men	Women	Children	Total	Men	Women	Children
	No.	No.	No.	No.	No.	No.	No.	No.
5½ years								
India	96310	33583	27948	34779	88041	26908	26720	34413
Pakistan	73474	27555	15036	30883	69055	23865	14588	30602
Jamaica	50924	5636	14048	31240	49414	4782	13561	31071
Rest of Caribbean	37553	8023	14377	15153	32864	5573	12687	14604
C'wealth West Africa	32767	15793	13698	3276	19628	6369	10405	2854
Cyprus	11445	3620	4288	3537	9253	2198	3632	3423
Rest of Commonwealth	82722	32622	28288	18212	53105	17997	20205	14903
Total	385195	130434	117683	137080	321360	87692	101798	131870
3¾ years								
India	62392	25321	17411	19660	56004	20088	16543	19383
Pakistan	44538	23344	7902	13292	42103	21460	7578	13065
Jamaica	36170	4855	12024	19291	35110	4226	11695	19189
Rest of Caribbean	27869	6653	11381	9835	24913	4835	10637	9431
C'wealth West Africa	27050	13603	11209	2238	16232	5768	8531	1933
Cyprus	9360	2937	3453	2970	7808	1901	3023	2884
Rest of Commonwealth	61610	27449	21028	13133	39992	14480	15147	10365
Total	268989	104162	84408	80419	222162	72758	73154	76250
1¾ years								
India	33918	8262	10537	15119	32037	6830	10177	15030
Pakistan	28936	4211	7134	17591	26952	2405	7101	17537
Jamaica	14754	781	2024	11949	14304	556	1866	11882
Rest of Caribbean	9684	1370	2996	5318	7961	738	2050	5173
C'wealth West Africa	5717	2190	2489	1038	3396	601	1874	921
Cyprus	2085	683	835	567	1445	297	609	539
Rest of Commonwealth	21112	8773	7260	5079	13113	3517	5058	4538
Total	116206	26270	33275	5666	99208	14944	28644	55620

Source Commonwealth Immigrants Acts Statistics.

Nearly 50 per cent of all persons who are likely to remain for the entire period since the beginning of the Commonwealth Immigrants Act are from India and Pakistan. The Caribbean countries account for another 25 per cent (see Table 32).

Table 32. Proportion of all Persons likely to remain by the six Groupings of Countries, 1962-7

	%
India	27·4
Pakistan	21·5
Jamaica	15·4
Rest of Caribbean	10·2
West Africa	6·1
Cyprus	2·6
Rest of Commonwealth	16·8
Total	100·0
Total Persons	321360

Source Commonwealth Immigrants Acts Statistics and authors' calculations.

Taking each category of immigrants, we determined the number of dependants that they ought to have (wherever they may be). Only women holders of vouchers, in our opinion, were likely to have their husbands in their country of origin. We assumed that each such female was married and a dependent male was expected. In 5½ years there were 10,414 such persons, but only 1,661 in the last period of 1¾ years or 960 persons as a mean for 1966 and 1967. Hence this is not a significant source of dependants.

The next step was to estimate the number of dependent females expected in respect of the male immigrants; this was done separately for each category of immigrants. In the case of long-term visitors, fewer women than men arrived. We would therefore expect that those females who have not arrived with their husbands will arrive as dependants in the future. From India there were 688 males and 555 females — therefore 133 females would be expected. In order to calculate the number of female dependants for male students, we assumed that 25 per cent of male students are married. Also, each male voucher holder is married and has a female dependant in his country of origin. Thus we estimate that for 5½ years, 62,488 dependent females would be expected, of whom only 7,712 would be for the last period of 1¾ years.

Finally, we estimated the number of children who ought to have arrived for each category of immigrants (except students). For this exercise we used three different proportions, which we defined as an absolute maximum, in which we assumed that each adult male immigrant ought to have four children at the time of arrival, and each female two children. Next is a high maximum assumption in which each male ought to have three children but each female only one child. Finally, a low maximum in which the male ought to have two children and the female one child. Students in each of the three ratios ought to have one child. When these ratios are multiplied, the number of children who have already arrived during the period is subtracted from the maximum number of children expected to give the actual number that ought to arrive.

From the first assumption we should expect 287,200 children; from the second, 208,900; from the third, 141,000. The evidence suggests that the last assumption is more realistic and we will thus use it for future reference. It is unlikely that women voucher holders, due to their skill and lower age group, could have, on average, more than one child. Most of these women appear to be single, to have had one child, or to have not yet started a stable married life. The majority of female student nurses are single. Male students who are married would not be expected to have children until their studies are completed. Other males we assumed to be, on average, 30 years old on arrival in Britain. Considering that not all of these are married, especially voucher holders, the average family size should not exceed on the average two children. If we were to make our calculations in respect of the coloured Commonwealth immigrant population, for the period preceding the 1962 Act, we would have used the second assumption. Considering that immigrants during the last two years, are, as a group, more urbanized, better educated and from a different socio-economic stratum, they would tend to have a lower fertility rate than previous immigrants.

The number of dependent persons who would normally be expected to arrive under 'male persons likely to remain' in England and Wales in 1967, in relation to each of the three ratios for the different periods is as follows:

Table 33. Number of Dependants who normally would be expected to arrive to all Adult Male Coloured Commonwealth Immigrants, June 1962 - December 1967

Periods	Adult males likely to remain	Absolute maximum	High maximum	Low maximum
5½ years	87600	360110	281750	213910
3¾ years	72700	313650	245590	186470
1¾ years	14900	46450	36160	27530

Source Commonwealth Immigrants Acts Statistics and authors' calculations.

Although the last 1¾ years represents a quarter of the period under review, it accounts for nearly one-eighth of the number of dependants who ought to arrive. Table 34 indicates the estimates for each coloured Commonwealth country. The steep fall in the latter period is a further indication of the extent of the completion of families in the host country and the expected tapering off of future arrivals.

Table 34. Three Assumptions of Dependants who ought to arrive

	Absolute Maximum								High Maximum								Low Maximum							
	Total Persons	%	Men	%	Women	%	Children	%	Total Persons	%	Men	%	Women	%	Children	%	Total Persons	%	Men	%	Women	%	Children	%
5½ years																								
India	110821		1921		19925		88975		87364		1921		19925		65518		65828		1921		19925		43982
Pakistan	108575		339		21378		86858		86573		339		21378		64856		64910		339		21378		43193
Jamaica	23762		2379		3010		18373		17680		2379		3010		12291		13977		2379		3010		8588
Rest of Caribbean	26297		2156		3453		20688		19734		2156		3453		14125		15327		2156		3453		9718
C'wealth West Africa	17641		177		3558		13906		14152		177		3558		10417		10840		177		3558		7105
Cyprus	8670		649		1225		6796		6474		649		1225		4600		5027		649		1225		3153
Rest of Commonwealth	64340		2793		9939		51608		49772		2793		9939		37040		37997		2793		9939		25265
Total	360106		10414		62488		287204		281749		10414		62488		208847		213906		10414		62488		141004
3¾ years																								
India	88751		1395		16362		70994		70131		1395		16362		52374		52906		1395		16362		35149
Pakistan	101423		249		20025		81149		80910		249		20025		60636		60659		249		20025		40385
Jamaica	21725		2208		2757		16760		16179		2208		2757		11214		12841		2208		2757		7876
Rest of Caribbean	23203		1883		2998		18322		17417		1883		2998		12536		13577		1883		2998		8696
C'wealth West Africa	16943		168		3374		13401		13571		168		3374		10029		10367		168		3374		6825
Cyprus	7858		572		1120		6166		5869		572		1120		4177		4569		572		1120		2877
Rest of Commonwealth	53747		2278		8140		43329		41512		2278		8140		31094		31555		2278		8140		21137
Total	313650		8753		54776		250121		245589		8753		54776		182060		186474		8753		54776		122945
1¾ years																								
India	22070		526		3563		17981		17233		526		3563		13144		12922		526		3563		8833
Pakistan	7152		90		1353		5709		5663		90		1353		4220		4251		90		1353		2808
Jamaica	2037		171		253		1613		1501		171		253		1077		1136		171		253		712
Rest of Caribbean	3094		273		455		2366		2317		273		455		1589		1850		273		455		1122
C'wealth West Africa	698		9		184		505		581		9		184		388		473		9		184		280
Cyprus	812		77		105		630		605		77		105		423		455		77		105		273
Rest of Commonwealth	10593		515		1799		8279		8260		515		1799		5946		6442		515		1799		4128
Total	46456		1661		7712		37083		36160		1661		7712		26787		27529		1661		7712		18156

Source Commonwealth Immigrants Acts Statistics.

According to the low maximum assumption the following is the distribution of persons who ought to have arrived to complete coloured Commonwealth immigrant households.

Table 35. According to Low Maximum: Distribution of Persons who ought to have arrived

	%
India	30·8
Pakistan	30·2
Jamaica	6·5
Rest of Caribbean	7·2
West Africa	5·1
Cyprus	2·4
Rest of Commonwealth	17·8
Total Commonwealth	100·0
Total persons	213900

Source Commonwealth Immigrants
Acts Statistics.

If we were to assume that all dependants who arrived during the 5½ year period were directly related to those adult immigrants who arrived during the same period, then it would have been possible to estimate the number of dependants expected to arrive. The difficulty is that there is no indication of the relationship of dependants to the year of arrival of their spouse or parents. This means that we cannot relate the arrival of dependants in any given year to the number of immigrants.

Table 36 below shows that 6,900 Indian, and 20,500 Pakistani dependants are expected to arrive to complete nuclear families of immigrants who arrived in the 5½ year period. For Jamaica, the rest of the Caribbean, West Africa and Cyprus, more dependants have arrived than the adult immigrants for this period. This means that dependants are arriving of immigrants from these countries who came to Britain before the passing of the Act in 1962. This situation may be accounted for by looking at the great number of immigrants from these countries who arrived just before the Act came into force. The result is that fewer dependants can be expected from those areas, and many more from India and Pakistan.

Voucher holders and their dependants in ten years time
The mean number of voucher holders who arrived in 1966 and 1967 is 4,933 persons, 80 per cent of whom were men. India alone accounts for 40 per cent of all male voucher holders. The mean distribution of all voucher holders by territories for the last two years is as follows: India 46·9 per cent, Pakistan 14·9 per cent, Jamaica 4·8 per cent, rest of the Caribbean 7·9 per cent, Cyprus 1·8 per cent, West Africa 0·9 per cent, and rest of the Commonwealth 22·8 per cent. These voucher holders ought to

Table 36. Future Arrival of Dependants according to the Commonwealth Immigrants Act (for immigrants who arrived 1962-7)

Country	Ought to Arrive	Arrived	To Arrive	Excess related to earlier immigrants
India	65828	58928	6900	
Pakistan	64910	44443	20467	
Jamaica	13997	37943		23966
Rest of Caribbean	15327	17380		2053
West Africa	10840	11107		267
Cyprus	5027	5471		444
Rest of Commonwealth	37997	21586	16411	
Total	213908	196858	43778	26730

Source Commonwealth Immigrants Acts Statistics.

have, according to our three maximum assumptions, 22,750, 17,800 and 13,830 dependants. The last assumption therefore gives us a ratio of 2·7 dependants for each voucher holder.

In ten years' time, the number of voucher holders will be 49,330, of whom 39,740 will be men and 9,590 women. Their dependants, according to the last assumption, should be:

Total persons	Men	Women	Children
138320	9590	39740	88990

Therefore, voucher holders and their dependants, who ought to arrive in ten years should be 187,650 persons, if the present trend continues unchanged (see Table 37). Hence the average annual flow of voucher holders and their dependants ought not to exceed 19,000 persons per annum, with India alone accounting for nearly 50 per cent.

Projections of future arrivals of dependants based on the 1966 Census

As with the estimates based on the arrivals under the first Commonwealth Immigrants Act, we are using the profile method for the projections which are based on the 10 per cent 1966 Census of England and Wales. It is most likely that all these dependants will arrive within ten years, with the majority within the first few years. Hence we are not alarmed that the arrivals for the first six months of 1968 exceed the numbers in the corresponding period of 1967. We would like, however, to underline the fact that the considerable number of Kenyan Asians who arrived in the United Kingdom during the first quarter of 1968 will add a new dimension to the problem of ascertaining future arrivals. We do not at present have sufficient information to calculate the numbers of dependants who may arrive as a result of those East African Asians who entered before the passing of the 1968 Commonwealth Immigration Act.

Table 37.   Projection of Voucher Holders and their Dependants for ten Years*

Country of Origin	Mean arrivals 1966-7			Persons who ought to arrive in ten years			
	Total Persons	Men	Women	Total Persons	Men	Women	Children
India	2305	2000	205	89150	23050	23050	43050
Pakistan	738	686	52	28920	7380	7380	14160
Jamaica	236	138	98	8460	2360	2360	3740
Cyprus	89	45	44	3120	1430	1430	1340
Rest of Caribbean	394	233	161	14150	3940	3940	6270
West Africa	49	43	6	1900	490	490	920
Other Commonwealth Countries	1122	829	293	41950	11220	11220	19510
Total	4933	3974	959	187650	49330	49330	88990

* Projection for other sources of dependants are summarised in Table 43.
Source   Commonwealth Immigrants Acts Statistics.

Since the total entries for the years 1965 to the passing of the Act amounted to 39,395 and since these undoubtedly included a considerable number of dependants as well as short-stay visitors, this group is unlikely to produce a very large number of dependants for future entry. Subsequent to the passing of the Act, entry is at present restricted to 1,500 voucher holders a year. However, the East African Asians have been excluded from our projections.

Future dependants of coloured Commonwealth immigrants based on the 1966 Census would be from three categories of the adult coloured population in the host country. First, dependants of married males who have no member of their family in England. Secondly, dependants of families which are partly completed, and thirdly, those belonging to persons under-enumerated in the 1966 Census about whom we know very little.

Married men without their Dependants
From the special tabulations of the 1966 Census, we have determined the number of married men without any member of their family in England. Since there is no reliable estimate of their number in each age group we assume their mean age is 30 years and that they ought to have either four, three, or two children at the time of their arrival, left behind in the country of origin. We shall discuss these alternative assumptions below.

Especially from Pakistan there should be substantial in-flows of female immigrants and children (see Table 38). If we take the mean arrivals for the last two years then for most countries all these dependants ought to arrive in less than five years.

Table 38. Dependants of Married Men without any Dependants in Host Country enumerated in the 1966 Census

		Children: three different maxima		
	Women	4	3	2
India	13900	55600	41700	27800
Pakistan	31300	125200	93900	62600
Jamaica	3600	14400	10800	7200
Rest of Caribbean	1700	6800	5100	3400
Cyprus	—	—	—	—
West Africa	3500	17000	10500	7000
Total	54000	219000	162000	108000

Source Commonwealth Immigrants Acts Statistics.

Dependants of under-enumerated Persons in 1966

We have already determined the number of persons under-enumerated in the 1966 10 per cent Sample Census of England and Wales, but we have no further information pertaining to their sex and age structure. The following calculations are based on the assumption that all the under-enumerated persons are adult males. Furthermore, according to a high maximum assumption 50 per cent are married and a low maximum assumption 25 per cent are married. It is our opinion that the latter assumption is more realistic than the first. Besides, we assume that these married persons have all their dependants in their country of origin. Also, each married person has two children and a wife.

According to the low maximum assumption, Table 39 below shows that 22,970 dependent wives and children ought to arrive to complete the family structure of Pakistani under-enumerated persons. For Jamaica and the rest of the Caribbean the numbers ought to be 12,980 and 10,360 dependants respectively. From India the total is nearly 8,300 persons but this is because only 11,000 persons were estimated to be under-enumerated. Therefore the total number of dependent wives and children from persons under-enumerated is nearly 60,000, which consists of 20,000 wives and 40,000 children.

Dependants of married couples

By assuming that each married household ought to have a certain maximum number of children we can determine the total who ought to be present in such households. We use the following proportions:

	No. of Children
15 - 19 years	1
20 - 24 ,,	1·5
25 - 44 ,,	2·5
45 - 49 ,,	1·5

Table 39. Dependants of Persons under-enumerated in 1966

Country	No. of persons under-enumerated	Wives		Children		Total Dependent Persons	
		High maximum	Low maximum	High maximum	Low maximum	High maximum	Low maximum
India	11090	5545	2772	11090	5540	17640	8320
Pakistan	30620	15310	7655	30620	15310	45930	22970
Jamaica	17310	8655	4327	17310	8650	25970	12980
Rest of Caribbean	13810	6905	3452	13810	6910	20720	10366
Rest of Commonwealth	7000	3400	1750	7000	3500	10500	5250
Total	72800	39000	20000	79800	40000	120000	59900

Source Special Tabulations.

We have assumed that married women in the 25-44 years age group ought to have 2·5 children and not 3 or more for the following reasons. Firstly, most of the children in households are born and remain in the host country, especially those under the age of 9 years. It would be expected that where most of the wives of families are housewives, they would have their children with them and not send them to their country of origin to be cared for by their grand-parents. This seems to be more noticeable among Indians and Pakistanis; among West Indian households where the employment rate among women is high the smaller children, for economic reasons, would be expected to be sent to their grand-parents or other relatives. We have already pointed out that this practice among West Indians does not involve a significant proportion of children born in this country. Table 3 of the special tabulations of the 1966 Census shows that the children under four years of age born in this country are in the majority in the five year age groups. Moreover, in the 5-9 years age group, the number of such children in households is a significant proportion of all children. Our estimate is that less than 10 per cent of all children born in the host country were sent to their parents' country of origin for economic or cultural reasons.

Having taken into account the consolidation of the nuclear family in the host country, we derived our second reason for the 2·5 children family to married women 25-44 years of age. Table 7 of the special tabulations indicates that the mean number of children for married women with children in households is less than 2·5, while for all married women, the mean is 1·5 children. We have therefore added one child to each married woman's family to derive the 2·5 children family. This increase of 40 per cent is nearly twice the actual Notting Hill Housing Survey figure, which is evidence that our assumption is not under-estimating the number of children in the 25-44 years age group among married women.

Thirdly, nearly 30 per cent of all married women have no children. As we have already pointed out in Chapter 3, this is typical of all the coloured Commonwealth nationalities in the U.K. This would reduce significantly the mean number of children per family. Other studies have pointed out that on the arrival of the wife in England, especially of Indians, no further member of her family is normally expected to be left behind. If this is so then it is further evidence for our profile assumptions.

Fourthly, in one and two children households, nearly 50 per cent of all children are over 5 years of age. The length of separation between husband and wife is one of the factors accounting for this phenomenon, but it is also an indication of family planning, which eventually results in a small-sized family.

The number in the 45-49 years age group declines because of children leaving home. Besides if there are children over 16 years of age not in the host country, then they would not be permitted to immigrate in accordance with the Commonwealth Immigrants Act. These are the main reasons why we consider that in this age group of married females, the mean number of children in the nuclear family ought to be 1·5.

It may be objected that the complete family sizes which can be inferred from maxima used in this section do not reflect adequately the high fertilities observed in immigrants' countries of origin, nor some of the sample surveys carried out in this country. It is perhaps therefore necessary to recapitulate some of the factors which have been responsible for scaling down the 'normal' family sizes of South East Asia and the Caribbean to the observed averages in the United Kingdom.

(1) The children observed here are the survivors of rather more births: those who died in infancy do not arrive here.

(2) There is probably a process of selection by which those with the very largest families are too encumbered to contemplate emigration.

(3) An increasingly high proportion of the immigrants since the 1962 Act are skilled and professional workers who would, in their own countries, have lower fertility.

(4) Not all children born in the immigrants' countries of origin are brought to the United Kingdom, either because their parents do not wish them to come, or because they are over the age-limits for dependants.

(5) There is also evidence that the immigrants settled here are beginning to approach British habits as regards age at marriage, and family planning workers report increasing interest in birth control amongst the immigrants.

(6) There is some evidence of children born to immigrant parents who are subsequently adopted or placed in children's homes, and therefore do not figure in households. Moreover, some of the children of West Indian parents who are born outside marriage, are frequently left in their country of origin with their grand-parents.

(7) There is often a prolonged period of separation of husband and wife, during their most fertile period, which reduces the total offspring of any union of a given duration. Similarly, we have to take into account the effect of common law unions on reducing the level of fertility. Judith Blake estimated that in Jamaica unstable unions account for 21 per cent loss of expected fertility.* Since unstable unions are more common among women under 30 years of age, we would expect West Indian female immigrants to have fewer children than their Asian counterparts. The profile concept of nuclear family size should not be confused with attained fertility. Our concept is based on the theoretical levels of fertility for age groups, which is adjusted to determine the number of children in families for such groups after taking into consideration the limitations that not all of them can be with their parents in the United Kingdom. Together with all these reasons, we must adopt fairly conservative maxima for the number of dependent children whom we shall ultimately expect in immigrant households.

The calculations for each country are indicated in Table 40. Rows 1-4 show the number of each country to each age group of married women. The number of children in row 3 for age group 25-44 is 78,910 for India, and 89,168 for Jamaica. Row 5 shows the total number of children who ought to be in each of the family profiles. Row 6 shows the number of children enumerated in the 1966 Census of England and Wales. Finally, row 7 indicates the number of children who ought to arrive to complete the existing nuclear families in the 1966 Census. Again we see that from India and Jamaica the numbers required, 20,440 and 15,500 children respectively, are very significant.

These profile assumptions result in a mean family size to all married females of 2·2 children, which is greater than the actual size according to the 1966 Census (see Table 41).

Dependants from three sources

We can now find the total of all dependants who ought to arrive to immigrants in England and Wales in 1966 to married men without any dependants living in the host country, persons under-enumerated in the census count, and incomplete nuclear families with the husband and wife living together but without all their children. If we subtract the actual arrival of dependants who arrived after the 1966 Census to December 1967, we have the final balance of dependants, wives and children who ought to arrive in 1968 and in the future (see Table 42).

The figures for India seem to be under-estimated by not more than 19,000. This may be attributed to the White Indian element in the immigrant population.

---

* Judith Blake et al., *Family Structure in Jamaica: The Social Context of Reproduction* (New York, Free Press of Glencoe, 1961).

Table 40. Children of Male Head of Households who ought to be in completed Households

Row	Age group of married females	Children in Household to age group	India married women	children	Pakistan married women	children	Jamaica married women	children	Rest of Caribbean married women	children	West Africa married women	children	Cyprus married women	children
1	15-19	1·0	1262	1262	253	253	523	523	404	404	292	292	407	407
2	20-24	1·5	7815	11723	1515	2268	5109	7664	4900	7350	3032	4548	2505	3758
3	25-44	2·5	31564	78910	5325	13313	35667	89168	23115	57788	6938	17348	10458	26145
4	45-59	1·5	12364	18546	706	1059	4766	7149	2853	4280	102	153	2735	4103
5	No. who ought to be in host country		53005	110441	7799	16893	46065	104504	31272	69822	10364	22341	16105	34413
6	Total at Census 1966			90000		17200		89000		63000		9500		31400
7	No. who ought to arrive			20441		—		15504		6822		12841		3013

Source Special Tabulations.

Table 41. Mean Number of Children per Married Woman in Households

	Census 1966	Profile Calculation Table 40	Profile Increase
India	1·7	2·1	0·4
Pakistan	2·2	2·3	0·1
Jamaica	1·9	2·3	0·4
Rest of Caribbean	2·1	2·2	0·1
West Africa	0·9	2·2	1·3
Cyprus	1·9	2·1	0·2

Source Special Tabulations and authors' calculations.

Table 42. Summary of Dependants who ought to arrive after 1967 according to the 1966 Census

	India		Pakistan		Jamaica		Rest of Caribbean	
Source of Dependants	women	children	women	children	women	children	women	children
Married men without any dependants	13900	27800	31300	62600	3600	7200	1700	3400
Estimate of dependants of under-enumerated persons	5272	5540	7655	15310	4327	8650	3452	6910
Incomplete nuclear families	–	20441	–	307	–	15504	–	6822
Total	19172	53781	38955	77604	7927	31354	5152	17132
Arrived after Census to December 1967	9052	14626	6763	17321	1016	11681	773	4937
To arrive after 1967	10120	39155	32192	60283	6911	19673	4379	12195
Total women and children	49300		92400		26600		16600	

* These estimates do not include the future arrivals of voucher holders and dependants. For these categories, the average annual estimates are given on pp. 46 and 47.

Source Commonwealth Immigrants Acts Statistics, Special Tabulations and authors' calculations.

Chapter 5 / Conclusion

We have spent a good deal of time in presenting all the available evidence on the size and composition of the existing coloured Commonwealth immigrant population of the United Kingdom.* This exercise has been undertaken in the hope that the figures presented here may serve as a basis for a somewhat more realistic forecast of the future immigrant population of the country than the rather wild guesses which have become widespread in recent years. Any forecast must, of course, be hedged around with a list of the uncertainties which remain, and it is as well to enumerate the main sources of error here, if only to show that there is not as much room for doubt as is often assumed.

First of all, the figures given in this monograph for the existing coloured population have to be amended to provide for under-enumeration. We have census figures for 1961 and 1966, we have passenger figures, and we have the returns under the Commonwealth Immigrants Acts. In this paper, we have taken the largest possible figures throughout, that is, we have used arrival figures to amend the census returns, and we believe the resulting total estimates of coloured Commonwealth immigrants in Great Britain to be reliable indicators. They are significantly smaller, however, than some of the figures published recently, but without any evidence as to the origin of the information. To our knowledge, none of the official or unofficial data available in 1968 can be held to prove more serious under-enumeration than we have allowed for in this report.

We examined the statistics relating to immigrants in 1951, 1961, and 1966, as they appear in the census reports. We have also analysed carefully the returns of arrivals and departures, and then reconciled the census figures with the known movements of persons between census dates. We have drawn also on special detailed tabulations of the 1966 Sample Census for London and the West Midlands conurbations. From all this information we have derived what we believe to be a true picture of the immigrant population by country of origin, sex and age. We have also both the Census and the data on 1,500 immigrant households provided by the 1967 Notting Hill survey to arrive at a figure for children born here to immigrant parents — a highly significant factor in estimating future immigration to complete families. We have shown that a

---

* This, in our definition, includes the Cypriots who have been included for practical purposes. We exclude non-Commonwealth non-whites of whom there are few in this country, mostly Arabs, and who are for legal purposes treated like any other aliens.

large proportion of children in these households were born in the United Kingdom (Table 27) and we have concluded that in many cases the current structure leaves little room for the supposition that many older children, born overseas, have yet to arrive.

We have built up 'profiles' for each immigrant group − that is to say, we have tried to estimate what kind of households ought to be associated with the known immigrants who came to this country either before the 1962 Act, or since that time. We found, both in the 1966 census and in the Notting Hill survey, that the great majority of Caribbean households were already existing as complete or nearly complete family units; the Pakistani group was the only one in which the degree of family re-union was low, and where there were still many wives who might be expected to join their husbands in Britain. From these calculations we were able to produce estimates of future arrivals. We have analysed all immigrants according to the nature of their permission to land, and have deducted from the total those who on past experience are likely to return to their own countries. A remarkable feature of all the statistics has been the evidence of a constant outflow. The history of migration in other countries of the world shows that the vast majority of immigrants leave their country to establish permanent residence abroad. The outflow rate in this country of coloured immigrants is considered to be remarkably high. In 1967, it is estimated that 14,000 coloured Commonwealth immigrants left Great Britain for permanent residence in other countries. The largest group of 4,200 migrants were West Indians, but they were followed by 5,000 Indians and Pakistanis. If this trend were to continue, we would expect that the inflow of immigrants, who would be mainly voucher holders and their dependants, would not be much greater than the outflow.

Apart from people with only temporary permission to stay in the United Kingdom, there are long-term visitors and students − both categories who might be expected at some future data to seek to stay in the United Kingdom permanently, but who, on present evidence, leave again in most cases after completing their studies or accomplishing their business.

Of those who may be expected to remain here (if work opportunities exist), we know that many are married, and have their wives with them. For those who are married and alone, we have then calculated that each may bring a wife. For those who are unmarried, we have allowed the arrival of a future wife (or a husband, since either sex may claim for an entry permit of an intended spouse). Such estimates are clearly already on the high side: many will never marry; others will marry those of their own ethnic group already in the United Kingdom and single; others will marry British wives or husbands.

Similarly, we have made very liberal allowances for the future arrivals of the children of those who are married and alone. (Their children can now only come if the mother also comes.) Our calculation has been based on the assumption that each 'complete' immigrant family will have five surviving children when the mother reaches the end of her child-bearing age. This is clearly an over-estimate if we take it as a basis for future arrivals. As we saw, many of the children must have been born before 1950 if their fathers married at the normal age of their country: if so, then if they were not here by 1967, they will not now come except as voucher holders.

Even if all children are under age, an average of five is an outside estimate. We know that the men who are in the United Kingdom and married, but alone, have been separated from their wives, sometimes for a considerable length of time: therefore their family size will be much smaller than the high maximum we have allowed. Analysis of complete immigrant families in the United Kingdom suggests that five children is a very high average even for those who have moved as complete families: our Notting Hill group had far fewer than that.

The disquiet about the future size of the immigrant population has been largely caused by the high rate of arrival of dependants in this country in the last two years. Our profiles clearly show that this cannot continue much longer, and that the peak must soon be passed. We saw that 72 per cent of all arrivals in 1967 were dependants. There were very few voucher-holders; and most of the rest were, legally at least, transients. According to our Table 43, no more than 223,000 women and children may be expected to arrive after the end of 1967. We may assume that voucher-holders who have arrived between the 1966 census (our latest base date) and the end of 1967 will in turn allow their dependants to come. Some of these will already be included in the returns before us, but making allowance for this, the total may still be expected to rise to 236,000 (see Table 42). If the rate of arrival in 1967 were maintained (48,000) all these people might be expected to arrive within the next five years.

We may summarise the position in 1968 by assuming that the total coloured population, together with all dependants legally entitled and likely to enter over the next few years, consists of the following:

Enumerated in 1966 census	727,000
Allowed for under-enumeration	81,000
Arrivals since 1966 census, April 1966 - December 1967	99,000
Dependants expected in respect of those already in this country at census date	223,000
Dependants estimated for voucher holders who arrived April 1966 - December 1967	13,000
Children born in this country to immigrant parents	263,000
Total	1,406,000

This estimate of course does not make any allowance for outflow, or for mortality and future births. Thus if all the dependants of the coloured Commonwealth immigrants were in Great Britain, their total population is estimated to be 1,406,000 persons at the end of 1967. If we include the children of immigrants who are over 16 and therefore not entitled to enter Britain under present law an additional 20,000 might be added; if 16-18 year olds were allowed to enter, an additional 12,000 might be added.

Table 43. Future Arrival of Dependants to Immigrants in England and Wales at December 1967

	Dependants expected to arrive after 1967						Dependants of Potential Immigrants* Apr. '66 - Dec. '67		Total Women and Children to arrive after 1967		Actual Arrivals 1967		Years required at the rate of 1967 for all dependants to arrive
	Women		Children		Total								
	No.	%	No.	%	No.	%	No.	%	No.	%	No.	%	No.
India	10120	15·8	39155	24·6	49300	22·1	6200	47·7	55500	23·5	14300	29·8	3·9
Pakistan	32192	50·3	60283	37·9	92500	41·4	2100	16·2	94500	40·0	17200	35·8	5·5
Jamaica	6911	10·8	19673	12·4	26600	12·0	500	3·8	27100	11·5	7800	16·3	3·5
Rest of Caribbean	4379	6·8	12195	7·7	16600	7·4	800	6·2	17400	7·4	3300	6·9	5·3
Rest of Commonwealth	10128	15·8	27492	17·3	38100	17·1	3400	26·2	41500	17·8	5800	12·1	7·2
Total	64000		159000		223000		13000		236000		48000		4·9

* Mainly voucher holders.

This study has tended to show that most immigrant families where both husband and wife are present cannot have many eligible dependants left in their home areas. It is likely that many of those who have in fact arrived are related to those husbands who were known, in 1966, to be without their wives, and of course to the under-enumerated population for which we have allowed in total, though since they are missing from the census we know less about their age and marital structure. The married men without wives are mostly the Pakistanis (nearly 25 per cent of the total Pakistani married men fall into that category), and the Indians come next, so that it is not surprising that these two nationalities are most strongly represented amongst the arrivals of wives, accounting for nearly 50 per cent of the total.

Where, then, do the uncertainties lie? So far we have only discussed the reasons why we believe the estimates presented in our tables to be on the high side, and why we do not believe there is much room for error about the present coloured Commonwealth-born population, or their future dependants.

First of all, we have largely omitted from our calculations the 1968 arrivals of East African Asians from whom we had not got complete returns when our statistics were compiled. It is possible that they, with their permissible dependants, might increase the total by 7,500.

Secondly, we have somewhat scanty information about those who arrived between the 1961 census and the coming into force of the Commonwealth Immigrants Act: their approximate numbers, sex, and ethnic groups are known from the Passenger Surveys, but their age and marital structure are not, and we have had to infer their peculiarities from the 1966 census, which, however, does not distinguish the Commonwealth citizens by the year of their arrival, If this group is more severely under-enumerated than others, then they represent a source of error: those who were here in 1961 were not subject to 100 per cent enumeration, but this would not affect our estimates for the family profiles in the analysis of the 1966 10 per cent census. The Survey of Race Relations estimates that 21,000 persons were under-enumerated in the total enumerated population of 171,800 West Indians. Those who arrived before the middle of 1962 were not subjected to detailed scrutiny at the point of entry, but the arrival during those fourteen months (estimated at 200,000) may conceivably be the source of somewhat greater future demands for dependants' permits. The reasoning behind this assumption is of course that in the last few months when there was a rush to beat the new legislation, rather more married men have come without their wives, and if they are also the ones who were most heavily under-enumerated in 1966 then we have under-estimated the proportion of dependants in respect of this group. However, such an error could not be large, and scarcely affect the total picture.

Thirdly, we have so far assumed legislation to remain at least as permissive as it is, and evasion not to become more common. There could of course be relaxations of the rules about what constitutes a dependant, and there could be more wholesale mis-statements about relationship made by new arrivals. Neither of these seems likely.

The anxieties so widely voiced will, if anything, lead to a tightening up of the law, and the vigilance of the immigration officers, as well as their experience, increase over time.

What of the issue of vouchers? A great many of the small number of vouchers go to the most highly qualified trained and professional categories. There is no sign whatever of any increase in voucher-holding arrivals. On the contrary we have observed that there is an increase in the reflux rate of professionally qualified persons.* From September 1962 to September 1964, 1,935 Commonwealth-born doctors entered with vouchers, but in the same period, 1,507 left Great Britain.

Then there are the students. Once again, one expects the trend to be downwards rather than upwards, especially as the result of the government's decision to charge overseas students rather high fees in universities and colleges, which may discourage many. The indications are that a steady trickle will continue, but no flood. Will there be any changes in the proportion of those who will seek to stay in this country? This depends on the economic situation in their home countries, but also, as in the case of the voucher holders, on the skills they can offer. It is unlikely that a high proportion, for instance, of Asian arts graduates will find it profitable to stay in the United Kingdom when the possession of a British degree often confers considerable advantages in their own countries. Our statistics do not reveal any trend towards an increasing retention in this country of temporary immigrants: about the same proportion seem to return each year. In any case they never formed a very large part of the total.

This leaves us only with the uncertainty already referred to in the first chapter – the intentions of the children already here. If they, including those born in Britain, are going to bring over their spouses from their or their parents' country of origin, this would increase the number of potential arrivals of dependants. As far as can be judged at present, this possibility (which of course involves the 'arranged' marriage) is greatest in the case of the Indians and Pakistanis, and smallest in the case of those coming from the Caribbean.

We have not taken into account the possibility of the arrivals of such immigrants, because theoretically, this is one loop-hole in the present legislation, which is capable of letting in large numbers of immigrants. In practice, it is highly unlikely to have any effect on the future number of arrivals.

Our survey did not seek, and cannot give definite answers to the question of the future size of the whole 'coloured' population in England. This would depend on future birth and death rates, the degree of intermarriage, the numbers re-migrating, as well as the numbers of new arrivals from the Commonwealth. What we have done is to give our view on the maximum potential arrivals which might be expected under present legislation. We shall soon have 1968 figures. These may then be compared with the core of our estimate, and according to whether they are larger or smaller, we shall have some notion about the relevance of our calculations. Preliminary figures for the earlier part of 1968 certainly do not suggest that we shall be far out.

* See Appendix 4.

Appendix 1

This appendix contains four sets of tables of special tabulations* made available to the Institute's Survey of Race Relations in Britain and used with their permission. Each set has six tables for each of the main groups of countries in the report.

Because of the process of multiplication from two conurbations to six conurbations and then to England and Wales, the figures may have an estimated error of +1% to − 1%. Numbers therefore are not rounded off. Percentages are those for two conurbations, London and the West Midlands. Figures for India and Pakistan include White Indians and White Pakistanis.

---

* Special Tabulations from 1966 Sample Census for London and West Midland conurbations, upgraded for England and Wales.

Table 1A. Persons born in India by Age, Sex and Marital Condition, and Percentage of Age Groups to each Total.

	Males Total		Males Single		Males Married		Females Total		Females Single		Females Married		Total Persons	
	No.	%	No.	%	No.	%	No.	%	No.	%	No.	%	No.	%
Total	129860	100·0	50978	100·0	76039	100·0	102357	100·0	33414	100·0	58211	100·0	232190	100·0
Widowed	1945	1·5					9099	8·9						4·7
Divorced	898	0·7					1633	1·6						1·1
0 - 4	2049	1·6	2049	4·0			2395	2·3	2395	7·2			4427	1·9
5 - 9	4937	3·8	4937	9·7			4767	4·7	4767	14·3			9683	4·2
10 - 14	8075	6·2	8075	15·8			6770	6·6	6770	20·3			14834	6·4
15 - 19	10584	8·2	10208	20·0	376	0·5	7118	6·9	5834	17·5	1262	2·2	17727	7·6
20 - 24	13932	10·7	8995	17·6	4917	6·3	13061	12·8	5181	15·5	7815	13·4	26943	11·6
25 - 44	62712	48·3	14308	28·1	47610	60·9	38902	38·0	4549	13·6	31564	54·2	101835	43·9
45 - 59	19789	15·2	1716	3·4	17194	22·0	17612	17·2	2090	6·3	12364	21·2	37351	16·1
60 - 64	3807	2·9	419	0·8	3095	3·9	3722	3·6	566	1·7	1921	3·3	7513	3·2
65+	3974	3·1	273	0·5	2845	3·6	8012	7·8	1262	3·8	1688	2·9	11875	5·1

Table 1B. Persons born in Pakistan by Age, Sex and Marital Condition, with Percentage of Age Groups in each Total.

	Males Total		Males Single		Males Married		Females Total		Females Single		Females Married		Total Persons	
	No.	%	No.	%	No.	%	No.	%	No.	%	No.	%	No.	%
Total	59148	100·0	16970	100·0	41819	100·0	13980	100·0	5476	100·0	8000	100·0	73130	100·0
Widowed	238	0·4					480	3·4					699	0·9
Divorced	119	0·2					26	0·2					145	0·2
0 - 4	1193	2·0	1193	7·0			933	6·7	933	17·0			2099	2·8
5 - 9	1791	3·0	1791	10·5			1716	12·3	1716	31·3			3449	4·7
10 - 14	3056	5·2	3056	18·0			1136	8·1	1136	20·7			4172	5·7
15 - 19	3341	5·6	2959	17·4	382	0·9	933	6·7	682	12·4	253	3·2	4269	5·8
20 - 24	5419	9·2	2196	12·9	3222	7·7	1766	12·6	252	4·6	1515	18·9	7163	9·8
25 - 44	37714	63·8	5180	30·5	32319	77·3	5955	42·6	556	10·1	5325	66·6	43801	59·9
45 - 59	5394	9·1	477	2·8	4893	11·7	1035	7·4	126	2·3	706	8·8	6440	8·8
60 - 64	811	1·4	48	0·3	716	1·7	252	1·8	26	0·5	151	1·9	1061	1·4
65+	429	0·7	72	0·4	287	0·7	252	1·8	50	0·9	50	0·6	676	0·9

Table 1C. Persons born in Jamaica by Age, Sex and Marital Condition, with Percentage of Age Groups in each Total

| | Males | | | | | | Females | | | | | | Total Persons | |
| | Total | | Single | | Married | | Total | | Single | | Married | | | |
	No.	%	No.	%	No.	%	No.	%	No.	%	No.	%	No.	%
Total	78330	100·0	27210	34·7	51582	100·0	73510	100·0	25201	100·0	46313	100·0	151839	100·0
Widowed	523	0·4					1377	1·8					1904	1·2
Divorced	464	0·6					620	0·8					1078	0·7
0 - 4	536	0·7	537	1·9			385	0·5	385	1·5			910	0·6
5 - 9	2622	3·3	2622	9·6			2768	3·8	2768	11·1			5348	3·5
10 - 14	4765	5·9	4765	17·5			5633	7·7	5633	22·4			10330	6·8
15 - 19	4504	5·6	4475	16·4	30		5343	7·3	4820	19·1	523	1·1	9784	6·4
20 - 24	5749	7·2	3722	13·7	2028	3·9	7974	10·8	2837	11·3	5109	11·0	13662	8·9
25 - 44	49714	62·3	9427	34·6	39828	77·2	43530	59·2	7064	28·0	35667	77·2	92304	60·8
45 - 59	10963	13·7	1536	5·6	9007	17·4	6652	9·0	1405	5·6	4723	10·2	17358	11·4
60 - 64	608	0·8	44	0·2	536	1·0	592	0·8	179	0·7	193	0·4	1190	0·8
65+	319	0·4	87	0·4	145	0·3	633	0·8	110	0·4	97	0·2	953	0·6

Table 1D. Persons born in the Rest of the Caribbean by Age, Sex and Marital Condition with Percentage of Age Groups in each Total

| | Males | | | | | | Females | | | | | | Total Persons | |
| | Total | | Single | | Married | | Total | | Single | | Married | | | |
	No.	%	No.	%	No.	%	No.	%	No.	%	No.	%	No.	%
Total	59848	100·0	24304	100·0	34951	100·0	56160	100·0	22553	100·0	31632	100·0	116007	100·0
Widowed	260	0·4					1283	2·3					1546	1·3
Divorced	333	0·6					591	1·1					925	0·8
0 - 4	651	1·1	651	2·6			504	0·9	504	2·2			1156	1·0
5 - 9	2850	4·8	2850	11·7			3156	5·6	3156	14·0			6012	5·2
10 - 14	4007	6·7	4007	16·5			4467	7·7	4467	19·2			8353	7·2
15 - 19	3400	5·7	3298	13·6	102	0·3	4050	7·2	3646	16·2	404	1·3	7457	6·4
20 - 24	5874	9·8	4007	16·5	1866	5·3	8892	15·9	3977	17·6	4900	15·5	14766	12·7
25 - 44	36745	61·4	8492	34·9	27964	80·0	29442	52·5	5635	25·0	23115	73·1	66187	57·0
45 - 59	5511	9·2	868	3·6	4398	12·6	4482	7·9	1009	4·5	2853	9·0	10001	8·6
60 - 64	521	0·9	116	0·5	377	1·1	663	1·2	159	0·7	288	0·9	1185	1·0
65+	289	0·5	14	0·1	246	0·7	533	1·0	130	0·6	72	0·2	823	0·7

Table 1E. Persons born in Commonwealth West Africa by Age, Sex and Marital Condition, with Percentage of Age Groups in Each Total

	Males						Females						Total Persons	
	Total		Single		Married		Total		Single		Married			
	No.	%	No.	%	No.	%	No.	%	No.	%	No.	%	No.	%
Total	22216	100·0	7209	100·0	14846	100·0	13760	100·0	3367	100·0	10363	100·0	35969	100·0
Widowed	90	0·4					29	0·2					118	0·4
Divorced	75	0·3												
0 - 4	435	1·9	435	6·0			423	3·1	423	12·6			859	2·4
5 - 9	869	3·9	869	12·1			598	4·3	598	17·7			1467	4·1
10 - 14	390	1·8	390	5·4			350	2·5	350	10·4			741	2·1
15 - 19	300	1·3	285	4·0	15	0·1	641	4·7	350	10·4	292	2·8	949	2·6
20 - 24	2217	9·9	1214	6·8	1004	6·8	3790	27·5	758	22·5	3032	29·2	6047	16·8
25 - 44	17243	77·6	3865	53·7	13258	89·3	7842	56·9	888	26·4	6938	66·9	25032	69·6
45 - 59	674	3·0	135	1·9	495	3·3	116	0·9			102	1·0	785	2·2
60 - 64														
65+	88	0·4	15	0·2	75	0·5							89	0·2

Table 1F. Persons born in Cyprus by Age, Sex, and Marital Condition, with Percentage of Age Groups in Each Total

	Males						Females						Total Persons	
	Total		Single		Married		Total		Single		Married			
	No.	%	No.	%	No.	%	No.	%	No.	%	No.	%	No.	%
Total	32180	100·0	11906	100·0	19959	100·0	27253	100·0	8845	100·0	16450	100·0	59187	100·0
Widowed	177	0·6					1552	5·7					1717	2·9
Divorced	139	0·4					395	1·4					530	0·9
0 - 4	329	1·0	329	2·8			446	1·6	446	5·0			770	1·3
5 - 9	2149	6·7	2149	18·0			1807	6·6	1807	20·4			3939	6·7
10 - 14	2288	7·1	2288	19·2			2240	8·2	2240	25·3			4633	7·8
15 - 19	2882	8·9	2832	23·8	50	0·3	2595	9·5	2188	24·7	407	2·5	5328	9·0
20 - 24	3502	10·9	2083	17·4	1416	7·1	3588	13·2	1183	13·4	2405	14·6	7057	11·9
25 - 44	15295	47·5	1832	15·4	13348	66·9	11654	42·8	814	9·2	10458	63·6	26841	45·3
45 - 49	4690	14·6	353	3·0	4247	21·3	3524	12·9	177	2·0	2735	16·6	8181	13·8
60 - 64	515	1·6	38	0·3	430	2·2	586	2·1	27	0·3	216	1·3	1098	1·9
65+	530	1·6	12	0·1	468	2·3	813	3·0	11	0·1	230	1·4	1339	2·2

Table 2A. Persons in Households with the Head born in India, with Percentage of Age Groups to each Total

	Males						Females						Total Persons	
	Total		Single		Married		Total		Single		Married			
	No.	%	No.	%	No.	%	No.	%	No.	%	No.	%	No.	%
Total	153038	100·0	77898	100·0	72645	100·0	134730	100·0	63217	100·0	62137	100·0	286330	100·0
Widowed	1673	1·1					8121	6·0					9704	3·4
Divorced	816	0·5					1252	0·9					2064	0·7
0 - 4	18492	12·1	18492	23·7			20260	15·0	20260	32·0			38776	13·4
5 - 9	12257	8·0	12259	15·7			11879	8·8	11879	18·8			24176	8·4
10 - 14	12090	7·9	12090	15·6			10735	8·0	10735	17·0			22878	7·9
15 - 19	13408	8·8	13010	16·7	397	0·5	9503	7·1	8077	12·8	1426	2·3	23007	7·9
20 - 24	13179	8·6	8492	11·0	4664	6·4	13823	10·3	4925	7·8	8856	14·3	27028	9·4
25 - 44	57608	37·6	11588	14·9	45245	62·3	41402	30·7	4298	6·8	36090	58·1	83765	29·2
45 - 59	18639	12·2	1400	1·8	16462	22·7	16545	12·3	1468	2·3	12355	19·9	99410	34·7
60 - 64	3641	2·4	376	0·5	3075	4·2	3433	2·6	519	0·8	1642	2·6	7086	2·5
65+	3724	2·4	189	0·2	2802	3·6	7148	5·3	1058	1·7	1771	2·9	10833	3·8

Source Table 2, 1966 Special Tabulations of 10 per cent sample Census of England and Wales.

Table 2B. Persons in Households with the Head born in Pakistan, with Percentage of Age Groups to each Total

	Males						Females						Total Persons	
	Total		Single		Married		Total		Single		Married			
	No.	%	No.	%	No.	%	No.	%	No.	%	No.	%	No.	%
Total	51700	100·0	18976	100·0	32439	100·0	21499	100·0	10145	100·0	10523	100·0	73199	100·0
Widowed	145	0·3					682	3·2					796	1·1
Divorced	145	0·3					151	0·7					289	0·4
0 - 4	4082	7·9	4082	21·5			3911	18·2	3911	37·2			7862	14·5
5 - 9	2673	5·2	2673	14·1			2599	12·1	2599	25·7			5186	9·6
10 - 14	2769	5·3	2769	14·6			1453	6·7	1413	14·0			4148	5·7
15 - 19	2769	5·3	2530	13·3	239	0·7	1212	5·6	859	8·5	353	3·3	3956	5·4
20 - 24	4536	8·8	1933	10·2	2602	8·0	2725	12·7	480	4·7	2245	21·3	7187	9·9
25 - 44	29622	57·3	4321	22·7	25109	77·4	7747	36·0	656	6·4	6889	65·5	37337	51·3
45 - 59	4344	8·4	549	2·9	3795	11·7	1337	6·2	177	1·7	883	8·4	5668	7·9
60 - 64	549	1·1	48	0·2	477	1·5	151	0·7	50	0·5	50	0·5	699	1·0
65	359	0·7	72	0·3	215	0·6	403	1·9			100	1·0	748	1·0

Table 2C. Persons in Households with the Head born in Jamaica, with Percentage of Age Groups to Each Total

| | Males | | | | | | Females | | | | | | Total Persons | |
| | Total | | Single | | Married | | Total | | Single | | Married | | | |
	No.	%	No.	%	No.	%	No.	%	No.	%	No.	%	No.	%
Total	115213	100·0	63181	100·0	51104	100·0	108172	100·0	58693	100·0	47965	100·0	221326	100·0
Widowed	492	0·4					991	0·9					1484	0·7
Divorced	434	0·4					523	0·2					951	0·4
0 - 4	24357	21·1	24357	38·5			23849	22·0	23838	40·6			47775	21·6
5 - 9	13338	11·6	13338	21·1			13661	12·6	13661	23·3			26999	12·1
10 - 14	6242	5·4	6242	9·9			6885	6·4	6885	11·8			13032	5·9
15 - 19	4547	3·9	4518	7·1	30	0·6	5164	4·8	4558	7·8	606	1·3	9645	4·4
20 - 24	5835	5·1	3765	6·0	2070	4·0	8057	7·5	2451	4·2	5578	11·6	13830	6·3
25 - 44	49193	42·7	9384	14·9	39374	77·0	43049	39·8	5783	9·8	36632	76·4	91310	41·3
45 - 59	10803	9·4	1477	2·3	8935	17·5	6652	6·1	1281	2·2	4861	10·1	17204	7·7
60 - 64	637	0·5	44	0·1	564	1·1	537	0·5	152	0·2	221	0·5	1161	0·5
65+	261	0·2	58	0·1	130	0·2	330	0·3	83	0·1	69	0·1	588	0·3

Table 2D. Persons in Households with the Head born in the Rest of the Caribbean, with Percentage of Age Groups to each Total

| | Males | | | | | | Females | | | | | | Total Persons | |
| | Total | | Single | | Married | | Total | | Single | | Married | | | |
	No.	%	No.	%	No.	%	No.	%	No.	%	No.	%	No.	%
Total	81620	100·0	47218	100·0	33808	100·0	77834	100·0	42657	100·0	33304	100·0	159583	100·0
Widowed	246	0·3					1225	1·2					1474	0·9
Divorced	347	0·4					1173	0·8					998	0·6
0 - 4	17822	21·8	17822	37·7			16832	21·6	16832	39·4			34686	21·7
5 - 9	9013	11·0	9013	19·1			8675	11·1	8675	20·3			17704	11·1
10 - 14	4499	5·5	4499	9·5			4986	6·4	4986	11·7			9495	5·9
15 - 19	3675	4·5	3559	7·5	116	0·3	3934	5·1	3473	8·1	461	1·4	6171	3·9
20 - 24	5642	6·9	3877	8·2	1764	5·2	8128	10·4	2767	6·5	5347	16·1	13787	8·6
25 - 44	34979	42·9	7508	15·9	27153	80·3	29802	38·2	4756	11·1	24398	73·3	64832	40·6
45 - 59	5266	6·5	840	1·8	4196	12·4	4280	5·5	966	2·3	2666	8·0	9552	5·9
60 - 64	449	0·5	86	0·2	333	1·0	605	0·8	101	0·2	303	0·9	1055	0·7
65+	275	0·3	14	0·1	246	0·7	591	0·7	101	0·2	130	0·4	868	0·5

Table 2E. Persons in Households with the Head born in Commonwealth West Africa, with Percentage of Age Groups to each Total

	Males Total No.	%	Males Single No.	%	Males Married No.	%	Females Total No.	%	Females Single No.	%	Females Married No.	%	Total Persons No.	%
Total	24179	100·0	9782	100·0	14217	100·0	17954	100·0	6181	100·0	11326	100·0	41809	100·0
Widowed	104						73						178	
Divorced	75						14						89	
0 - 4	3386	14·0	3386	34·6			2959	16·8	2959	47·8			6363	15·2
5 - 9	1229	5·1	1229	12·6			1108	6·3	1108	17·9			2343	5·6
10 - 14	480	2·0	480	4·9			511	2·9	511	8·3			993	2·4
15 - 19	270	1·1	255	2·6	15	0·1	584	3·4	234	3·8	350	3·1	860	2·1
20 - 24	1977	8·2	1079	11·0	899	6·3	3695	21·0	612	9·9	3076	27·2	5711	1·4
25 - 44	16045	66·4	3221	32·9	12703	89·4	8440	47·9	699	11·3	7696	67·9	24475	58·5
45 - 59	674	2·8	120	1·2	509	3·6	262	1·5	44	0·7	189	1·7	935	2·2
60 - 64	15	0·1			15	0·1	14	0·1			14	0·1	29	0·1
65+	105	0·4	15	0·1	75	0·5	29	0·2	14	0·2			133	0·3

Table 2F. Persons in Households with the Head born in Cyprus, with Percentage of Age Groups to Each Total

	Males Total No.	%	Males Single No.	%	Males Married No.	%	Females Total No.	%	Females Single No.	%	Females Married No.	%	Total Persons No.	%
Total	43317	100·0	23396	100·0	19591	100·0	42088	100·0	20165	100·0	20064	100·0	85052	100·0
Widowed	190						1489						1666	
Divorced	151						369						578	
0 - 4	5915	13·7	5915	25·3			6031	14·3	6031	29·9			11894	13·9
5 - 9	5562	12·8	5562	23·8			4872	11·6	4872	24·2			10391	12·2
10 - 14	3703	8·5	3703	15·8			3817	9·1	3817	18·9			7488	8·8
15 - 19	3539	8·2	3488	14·9	50	0·3	3295	7·8	2748	13·6	547	2·7	6806	8·0
20 - 24	3704	8·5	2275	9·7	1416	7·2	4491	10·7	1399	6·9	3067	15·3	8157	9·6
25 - 44	15079	34·8	1985	8·5	12981	66·3	13843	32·9	1031	5·1	12507	62·3	28801	33·9
45 - 59	4664	10·8	379	1·6	4184	21·4	4147	9·9	204	1·0	3320	16·5	8775	10·3
60 - 64	543	1·3	50	0·2	442	2·3	662	1·6	26	0·1	267	1·3	1199	1·4
65+	619	1·3	38	0·1	518	2·6	929	2·2	38	0·2	356	1·8	1540	1·8

Table 3A.   Children in Households with the Head born in India, by Age and Sex, with Percentage of each Age Group to Total Persons

Age of Child		Total Persons		Males	Females
		No.	%	No.	No.
Total under	21	90770	100·0	45392	45247
Total under	1	8450	9·3	3954	4492
Total age	1	8172	9·0	3974	4190
„	„ 2	7404	8·2	3555	3845
„	„ 3	7492	8·3	3828	3651
„	„ 4	6939	7·7	3032	3909
„	„ 5	5087	5·6	2572	2505
„	„ 6	5491	6·0	2825	2656
„	„ 7	4427	4·9	2092	2333
„	„ 8	4300	4·8	2218	2073
„	„ 9	4640	5·1	2426	2203
„	„ 10	4235	4·7	2196	2031
„	„ 11	4788	5·3	2302	2484
„	„ 12	4363	4·8	2049	2311
„	„ 13	4363	4·8	2385	1965
„	„ 14	4256	4·7	2552	1684
„	„ 15	2235	2·5	1339	885
„	„ 16	1872	2·1	1003	865
„	„ 17	809	0·9	480	324
„	„ 18	405	0·4	126	280
„	„ 19	447	0·5	230	216
„	„ 20	595	0·6	250	346

Table 3B. Children in Households with the Head born in Pakistan, by Age and Sex with Percentage of each Age Group to Total Persons

		Total Persons		Males	Females
Age of Child		No.	%	No.	No.
Total under 21		17497	100·0	9452	8000
Total under 1		1689	9·8	859	859
Total age 1		1784	10·4	1003	807
,, ,, 2		1616	9·4	908	732
,, ,, 3		1278	7·4	549	757
,, ,, 4		1327	7·7	960	682
,, ,, 5		1134	6·6	644	505
,, ,, 6		1110	6·5	596	550
,, ,, 7		1061	6·2	429	656
,, ,, 8		989	5·8	621	379
,, ,, 9		819	4·8	382	455
,, ,, 10		796	4·6	477	327
,, ,, 11		699	4·1	406	303
,, ,, 12		723	4·2	429	303
,, ,, 13		723	4·2	501	227
,, ,, 14		603	3·5	382	227
,, ,, 15		410	2·4	310	100
,, ,, 16		120	0·7	48	76
,, ,, 17		169	0·9	143	26
,, ,, 18		73	0·4	23	50
,, ,, 19		24	0·1	23	—
,, ,, 20		47	0·2	48	—

Table 3C. Children in Households with the Head born in Jamaica, by Age and Sex, with Percentage of each Age Group to Total Persons

Age of Child	Total Persons No.	%	Males No.	Females No.
Total under 21	88725	100·0	44486	44853
Total under 1	9421	10·6	4706	4792
Total age 1	9295	10·5	4678	4696
,, ,, 2	10429	11·8	5257	5260
,, ,, 3	9757	11·0	5112	4737
,, ,, 4	8328	9·4	4315	4090
,, ,, 5	6299	7·1	3273	2947
,, ,, 6	6061	6·8	2983	3126
,, ,, 7	5515	6·2	2751	2809
,, ,, 8	4564	5·1	2187	2410
,, ,, 9	4018	4·5	2056	1997
,, ,, 10	2939	3·3	1259	1694
,, ,, 11	2393	2·7	1317	1101
,, ,, 12	2617	2·9	1303	1336
,, ,, 13	2352	2·6	1086	1281
,, ,, 14	2478	2·8	1173	1184
,, ,, 15	1063	1·2	420	647
,, ,, 16	825	0·9	377	454
,, ,, 17	281	0·3	102	179
,, ,, 18	154	0·2	87	69
,, ,, 19	42	—	30	14
,, ,, 20	28	—	14	14

Table 3D. Children in Households with the Head born in the Rest of the Caribbean, by Age and Sex, with Percentage of each Age Group to Total Persons

Age of Child	Total Persons		Males	Females
	No.	%	No.	No.
Total under 21	63286	100·0	31956	31272
Total under 1	6864	10·9	3559	3300
Total age 1	7400	11·5	3414	3977
,, ,, 2	7024	11·1	3733	3286
,, ,, 3	7038	10·9	3588	3444
,, ,, 4	5926	9·4	3312	2608
,, ,, 5	4640	7·3	2430	2205
,, ,, 6	3931	6·2	1997	1931
,, ,, 7	3410	5·4	1837	1571
,, ,, 8	3280	5·2	1504	1773
,, ,, 9	2197	3·5	1143	1052
,, ,, 10	2053	3·2	998	1052
,, ,, 11	2168	3·5	954	1211
,, ,, 12	1589	2·5	824	764
,, ,, 13	1705	2·7	738	966
,, ,, 14	1648	2·6	824	821
,, ,, 15	968	1·5	433	533
,, ,, 16	693	1·1	361	331
,, ,, 17	347	0·5	174	173
,, ,, 18	173	0·3	86	86
,, ,, 19	101	0·2	—	101
,, ,, 20	101	0·2	44	58

Table 3E. Children in Households with the Head born in Commonwealth West Africa, by Age and Sex, with Percentage of each Age Group to Total Persons

Age of Child		Total Persons		Males	Females
		No.	%	No.	No.
Total under	21	9486	100·0	5034	4431
Total under	1	2238	23·6	1259	977
Total age	1	1690	17·8	809	992
,, ,,	2	859	9·1	465	393
,, ,,	3	801	8·4	360	438
,, ,,	4	637	6·7	405	233
,, ,,	5	697	7·3	315	379
,, ,,	6	459	4·8	285	175
,, ,,	7	400	4·2	240	160
,, ,,	8	370	3·9	180	350
,, ,,	9	355	3·8	195	160
,, ,,	10	178	1·8	89	87
,, ,,	11	237	2·5	105	132
,, ,,	12	193	2·0	120	73
,, ,,	13	162	1·7	45	117
,, ,,	14	104	1·1	60	44
,, ,,	15	29	0·3	30	—
,, ,,	16	15	0·2	15	—
,, ,,	17	15	0·2	15	—
,, ,,	18	—	—	—	—
,, ,,	19	15	0·2	15	—
,, ,,	20	29	0·3	30	—

Table 3F. Children in Households with the Head born in Cyprus, by Age and Sex, with Percentage of each Age Group to Total Persons

	Total Persons		Males	Females
Age of Child	No.	%	No.	No.
Total under 21	31415	100·0	16255	15293
Total under 1	2373	7·6	1150	1234
Total age 1	2373	7·6	1327	1055
,, ,, 2	2083	6·6	1112	980
,, ,, 3	2827	9·0	1162	1680
,, ,, 4	2210	7·0	1150	1069
,, ,, 5	2133	6·8	1061	1081
,, ,, 6	2462	7·8	1162	1310
,, ,, 7	2020	6·4	1226	802
,, ,, 8	1894	6·0	1087	814
,, ,, 9	1831	5·8	1011	827
,, ,, 10	1742	5·5	859	890
,, ,, 11	1843	5·9	859	992
,, ,, 12	1414	4·5	657	764
,, ,, 13	1125	3·6	607	521
,, ,, 14	1275	4·1	670	611
,, ,, 15	707	2·3	417	293
,, ,, 16	442	1·4	278	165
,, ,, 17	290	0·1	202	89
,, ,, 18	177	–	113	63
,, ,, 19	76	–	63	12
,, ,, 20	113	–	76	38

Table 4A. Dependent Children in Households in Age Groups with the Head of Household born in India, Pakistan and Jamaica, with Percentage of Number of Children in each Age Group by Size of Household

| | Households | | No. of Children aged | | | | | | | | | |
| | | | 0-4 | | 5-9 | | 10-14 | | 15+ | | Total | |
	No.	%	No.	%	No.	%	No.	%	No.	%	No.	%
India												
All dependent children	76808	100·0	38457	100·0	23942	100·0	22006	100·0	6449	100·0	90854	100·0
0	38118	49·6										
1	12855	16·7	6236	16·2	1936	8·1	2072	14·2	1554	24·1	12855	14·1
2	11854	14·0	10918	28·4	5938	24·8	4874	22·1	1980	30·7	23708	26·0
3	7086	6·5	8385	21·8	6215	25·9	5299	24·1	1362	21·1	21261	23·4
4	3682	4·8	5575	14·5	4321	18·0	4150	18·9	682	10·6	14728	16·2
5+	3213	4·2	7342	19·1	5533	23·1	4555	20·7	872	13·5	18302	20·1
Pakistan												
All dependent children	19898	100·0	7694	100·0	5113	100·0	3546	100·0	868	100·0	17241	100·0
0	12422	58·8										
1	2629	13·2	1398	18·2	482	9·4	459	12·9	289	33·3	2629	15·1
2	2219	11·2	2195	28·5	1303	20·8	821	23·1	120	13·9	4438	25·4
3	1351	6·8	1857	30·4	1158	22·6	821	23·1	217	25·0	4053	23·2
4	772	3·9	302	16·9	1134	22·2	555	15·6	96	11·1	3087	17·7
5+	506	2·7	941	12·2	1038	20·3	892	25·0	145	1·6	3014	17·3
Jamaica												
All dependent children	54887	100·0	47230	100·0	26456	100·0	12780	100·0	2408	100·0	88875	100·0
0	19318	35·2										
1	10723	19·5	6621	14·0	1890	7·1	1750	13·7	462	19·2	10723	12·1
2	9981	18·2	12136	25·7	4550	17·2	2813	22·0	742	30·8	20242	22·8
3	6999	12·8	12039	25·5	6061	22·9	2464	19·3	434	18·0	20998	23·6
4	4143	7·5	7853	16·6	6173	23·3	2212	17·3	336	13·9	16574	18·7
5+	2184	3·9	8581	16·5	7658	29·4	3542	27·7	434	18·0	20340	16·5

Table 4B. Dependent Children in Households in Age Groups with the Head of Household born in the Rest of the Caribbean, C'wealth West Africa and Cyprus, with the Percentage of Number of Children in each Age Group by Size of Households

	Households		No. of Children aged									
			0-4		5-9		10-14		15+		Total	
	No.	%	No.	%	No.	%	No.	%	No.	%	No.	%
Rest of the Caribbean												
All dependent children	43370	100·0	34280	100·0	17458	100·0	9162	100·0	2500	100·0	63401	100·0
0	16346	37·7										
1	8845	20·4	5636	16·4	1431	8·1	1156	12·6	622	24·9	8845	14·0
2	8454	19·5	10969	31·9	3656	20·9	1764	19·6	520	20·1	16909	26·7
3	4725	10·7	8223	28·2	3873	22·2	1575	17·1	506	20·2	14177	22·4
4	2876	6·6	4942	14·2	4292	24·6	2024	22·0	246	9·8	11503	19·2
5+	2124	4·9	4509	13·4	4205	24·1	2644	28·9	607	24·3	11966	18·9
C'wealth West Africa												
All dependent children	16480	100·0	6225	100·0	2267	100·0	874	100·0	133	100·0	9515	100·0
0	11382	69·1										
1	2786	16·9	2327	37·3	266	11·8	118	13·6	73	55	2786	29·2
2	1125	5·9	1586	25·5	415	18·3	89	10·2	15	·11	2253	23·7
3	608	3·6	1111	17·9	474	20·9	193	22·0	44	33	1823	19·2
4	311	1·9	548	8·8	430	18·9	266	30·5	—		1245	13·1
5+	266	1·6	652	10·5	548	24·2	208	23·7	—		1408	14·8
Cyprus												
All dependent children	21389	100·0	11868	100·0	10341	100·0	7399	100·0	1881	100·0	31490	100·0
0	7351	36·5										
1	4700	24·9	2285	19·2	884	8·5	959	12·9	568	30·2	4698	14·9
2	5266	27·9	4204	35·4	3497	33·9	2248	30·4	581	30·8	10530	33·4
3	2841	15·1	2828	23·8	3207	31·0	2096	28·3	391	20·8	8522	27·1
4	1124	5·9	1527	12·9	1503	14·5	1237	16·7	227	12·1	4495	14·3
5+	581	3·1	1023	8·6	1250	12·1	858	11·6	113	6·0	3245	10·3

74

Appendix 2

The table in this appendix is a summary of detailed tables based on the Commonwealth Immigrants Acts, Statistics for 1962-7.

Table 1.   Potential Immigrants and their Dependants from 1962-7

| | Actual Arrivals | Likely to Remain | Dependants ought to have arrived 3 maxima assumptions | | |
			4 : 2 : 1 absolute	3 : 1 : 1 high	2 : 1 : 1 low
India	*No.*	*No.*	*No.*	*No.*	*No.*
5½ years June 1962 - December 1967					
Long-term Visitors	3112	1533	2595	1907	1219
Students	8920	2230	860	860	860
Holders of Vouchers	21242	21242	102368	81126	61805
Dependants	58928	58928	—	—	—
Others for Settlement	4108	4108	5008	3471	1944
Total	96310	88041	110821	87364	65828
3¾ years June 1962 - April 1966					
Long-term Visitors	2546	1533	2595	1907	1219
Students	7166	1791	700	700	700
Holders of Vouchers	17242	17242	83420	66178	50331
Dependants	33088	33088	—	—	—
Others for Settlement	2350	2350	2036	1346	656
Total	62392	56004	88751	70131	52906
1¾ years April 1966 - December 1967					
Long-term Visitors	556	—	—	—	—
Students	1754	439	160	160	160
Holders of Vouchers	4000	4000	18948	14948	11474
Dependants	25840	25840	—	—	—
Others for Settlement	1758	1758	2962	2125	1288
Total	33918	32037	22070	17233	12922

Pakistan	Actual Arrivals	Likely to Remain	Dependants ought to have arrived 3 maxima assumptions		
			4 : 2 : 1	3 : 1 : 1	2 : 1 : 1
	No.	No.	No.	No.	No.
5½ years June 1962 - December 1967					
Long-term Visitors	1297	754	1754	1336	918
Students	5168	1292	539	539	539
Holders of Vouchers	21208	21208	105362	84144	63285
Dependants	44443	44443	–	–	–
Others for Settlement	1358	1358	920	544	168
Total	73474	69055	108575	86573	64910
3¾ years June 1962 - April 1966					
Long-term Visitors	1090	754	1754	1336	918
Students	2765	666	248	248	248
Holders of Vouchers	19914	19914	99072	79248	59493
Dependants	19948	19948	–	–	–
Others for Settlement	821	821	349	168	–
Total	44538	42103	101423	80910	60659
1¾ years April 1966 - December 1967					
Long-term Visitors	207	–	–	–	–
Students	2403	626	291	291	291
Holders of Vouchers	1294	1294	6290	4996	3792
Dependants	24495	24495	–	–	–
Others for Settlement	537	537	571	376	168
Total	28936	26952	7152	5663	4251
Jamaica					
5½ years June 1962 - December 1967					
Long-term Visitors	1280	754	1026	767	508
Students	2880	1896	87	87	87
Holders of Vouchers	5164	5164	21062	15898	13013
Dependants	37943	37943	–	–	–
Others for Settlement	3657	3657	1587	928	269
Total	50924	49414	23762	17680	13977

| | Actual Arrivals | Likely to Remain | Dependants ought to have arrived 3 maxima assumptions | | |
			4 : 2 : 1 absolute	3 : 1 : 1 high	2 : 1 : 1 low
Jamaica—continued	No.	No.	No.	No.	No.
3¾ years June 1962 - April 1966					
Long-term Visitors	1062	754	1026	767	508
Students	2070	1318	72	72	72
Holders of Vouchers	4752	4752	19344	14592	12048
Dependants	25105	25105	—	—	—
Others for Settlement	3181	3181	1283	748	213
Total	36170	35110	21725	16179	12841
1¾ years April 1966 - December 1967					
Long-term Visitors	218	—	—	—	—
Students	810	578	15	15	15
Holders of Vouchers	412	412	1718	1306	1065
Dependants	12838	12838	—	—	—
Others for Settlement	476	476	304	180	56
Total	14754	14304	2037	1501	1136
Rest of Caribbean					
5½ years June 1962 - December 1967					
Long-term Visitors	3127	2107	2455	1753	1051
Students	9010	5341	234	234	234
Holders of Vouchers	5393	5393	22653	17260	14023
Dependants	17380	17380	—	—	—
Others for Settlement	2643	2643	955	487	19
Total	37553	32864	26297	19734	15327
3¾ years June 1962 - April 1966					
Long-term Visitors	2653	2107	2455	1753	1051
Students	6736	4326	175	175	175
Holders of Vouchers	4705	4705	19759	5054	12232
Dependants	11599	11599	—	—	—
Others for Settlement	2176	2176	814	435	19
Total	27869	24913	23203	17417	13477
1¾ years April 1966 - December 1967					
Long-term Visitors	474	—	—	—	—
Students	2274	1015	59	59	59
Holders of Vouchers	688	688	2896	2206	1791
Dependants	5781	5781	—	—	—
Others for Settlement	467	467	141	52	—
Total	9684	7951	3094	2317	1850

	Actual Arrivals	Likely to Remain	Dependants ought to have arrived 3 maxima assumptions		
			4 : 2 : 1 absolute	3 : 1 : 1 high	2 : 1 : 1 low
Cyprus	No.	No.	No.	No.	No.
5½ years June 1962 - December 1967					
Long-term Visitors	859	430	547	320	193
Students	2351	588	181	181	181
Holders of Vouchers	1761	1761	7507	5746	4634
Dependants	5471	5471	–	–	–
Others for Settlement	1003	1003	435	227	19
Total	11445	9253	8670	6474	5027
3¾ years June 1962 - April 1966					
Long-term Visitors	677	430	547	320	193
Students	1740	435	133	133	133
Holders of Vouchers	1605	1605	6881	5276	4243
Dependants	4526	4526	–	–	–
Others for Settlement	812	812	297	140	–
Total	9360	7808	7858	5869	4569
1¾ years April 1966 - December 1967					
Long-term Visitors	182	–	–	–	–
Students	611	153	48	48	48
Holders of Vouchers	156	156	626	470	391
Dependants	945	945	–	–	–
Others for Settlement	191	191	138	187	19
Total	2085	1445	812	605	458
C'wealth West Africa					
5½ years June 1962 - December 1967					
Long-term Visitors	2575	1194	2766	2106	1446
Students	15677	3919	1344	1344	1344
Holders of Vouchers	2704	2704	13166	10462	7935
Dependants	11107	11107	–	–	–
Others for Settlement	704	704	365	240	115
Total	32767	19628	17641	14152	10840
3¾ years June 1962 - April 1966					
Long-term Visitors	2184	1194	2766	2106	1446
Students	13104	3276	1141	1141	1141
Holders of Vouchers	2624	2624	12784	10160	7704
Dependants	8593	8593	–	–	–
Others for Settlement	545	545	252	164	76
Total	27050	16232	16943	13571	10367

C'wealth West Africa–continued	Actual Arrivals	Likely to Remain	Dependants ought to have arrived 3 maxima assumptions		
			4 : 2 : 1 absolute	3 : 1 : 1 high	2 : 1 : 1 low
	No.	No.	No.	No.	No.
1¾ years April 1966 - December 1967					
Long-term Visitors	391	–	–	–	–
Students	2573	643	203	203	203
Holders of Vouchers	80	80	382	302	231
Dependants	2516	2514	–	–	–
Others for Settlement	159	159	113	76	39
Total	5717	3396	698	581	473
Rest of Commonwealth					
5½ years June 1962 - December 1967					
Long-term Visitors	10164	4686	9570	7194	4818
Students	35941	11802	2086	2086	2086
Holders of Vouchers	10771	10771	48269	37498	29520
Dependants	21586	21586	–	–	–
Others for Settlement	4260	4260	4415	2994	1573
Total	82722	53105	64340	49772	37997
3¾ years June 1962 - April 1966					
Long-term Visitors	8539	4686	9570	7194	4818
Students	26415	8651	1454	1454	1454
Holders of Vouchers	8831	8831	39599	30768	24215
Dependants	14570	14570	–	–	–
Others for Settlement	3255	3254	3124	2096	1068
Total	61610	39992	53747	41512	31555
1¾ years April 1966 - December 1967					
Long-term Visitors	1625	–	–	–	–
Students	9526	3151	632	632	632
Holders of Vouchers	1940	1940	8670	6730	5305
Dependants	7016	7016	–	–	–
Others for Settlement	1005	1006	1291	898	505
Total	21112	13113	10593	8260	6442

Appendix 3

The table in this appendix gives in detail the categories of potential immigrants by their country of origin, and is based on the Commonwealth Immigrants Acts Statistics for 1962-7.

Table 1.   Categories of Potential Immigrants by Country of Origin.

	Long-Term Visitors				Students			
	Total Persons	Men	Women	Children	Total Persons	Men	Women	Children
	No.	No.	No.	No.	No.	No.	No.	No.
India								
1962	456	255	130	71	1529	1336	161	32
1963	834	435	285	114	2085	1764	237	84
1964	696	367	220	109	2015	1715	220	80
1965	469	234	158	77	1241	1055	139	47
1966	370	234	118	18	1182	955	175	52
1967	287	186	79	22	868	711	125	32
Total	3112	1711	990	411	8920	7536	1057	327
Pakistan								
1962	160	91	41	28	707	632	55	20
1963	420	189	119	112	1158	1017	90	51
1964	332	158	95	79	1206	1074	96	36
1965	154	70	37	47	596	537	42	17
1966	94	62	21	11	791	709	65	17
1967	137	76	36	25	710	647	48	15
Total	1297	646	349	302	5168	4616	396	156
Jamaica								
1962	178	63	89	26	343	161	164	18
1963	450	112	231	107	463	161	274	28
1964	281	86	139	56	696	246	426	24
1965	126	56	52	18	424	126	281	17
1966	108	38	56	14	499	146	346	7
1967	137	47	58	32	437	90	318	29
Total	1289	402	625	253	2862	1030	1809	123

Voucher Holders			Dependants				Others for Settlement			
Total Persons	Men	Women	Total Persons	Men	Women	Children	Total Persons	Men	Women	Children
No.	No.	No.	No.	No.	No.	No.	No.	No.	No.	No.
646	564	82	1565	46	659	860	645	114	264	267
8366	8085	281	6616	235	2803	3578	501	124	205	172
3828	3391	437	8770	329	3571	4870	435	129	188	118
3794	3282	512	12798	502	5202	7094	539	225	207	107
2433	2100	333	13357	856	4887	7614	918	391	288	239
2175	1899	276	15822	1520	5387	8915	1070	544	319	207
21242	19321	1921	60127	3488	22509	32931	4108	1527	1471	1110
391	381	10	505	12	204	289	210	16	97	97
13526	13461	65	3304	139	1186	1979	261	48	88	125
3296	3212	84	7046	241	2021	4784	180	47	41	92
2520	2443	77	6763	204	2644	3915	118	49	27	42
721	671	50	9319	165	2944	6210	205	83	47	75
754	701	53	17506	287	4555	12664	384	133	98	153
21208	20869	339	44443	1048	13554	29841	1358	376	398	584
903	485	418	2570	87	1118	1365	1030	84	574	372
1323	734	589	5522	150	2011	3361	685	100	337	248
1253	643	610	7877	230	1842	5805	844	138	531	175
1213	647	566	7480	216	1137	6127	467	101	326	40
237	138	99	6622	71	647	5904	218	48	84	86
235	138	97	7872	88	531	7253	313	88	97	128
5164	2785	2379	37943	842	7286	29815	3557	659	1949	1049

	Long-Term Visitors				Students			
	Total Persons No.	Men No.	Women No.	Children No.	Total Persons No.	Men No.	Women No.	Children No.
Rest of Caribbean								
1962	395	138	179	78	1061	437	522	102
1963	858	280	406	172	1521	552	854	115
1964	757	221	393	143	2027	605	1293	129
1965	452	168	218	66	1630	435	1116	79
1966	367	110	194	63	1707	472	1191	44
1967	200	60	107	33	994	299	642	53
Total	3029	977	1497	553	9040	2900	5598	512
C'wealth West Africa								
1962	395	164	174	57	2335	1692	580	63
1963	723	385	247	91	3733	2741	908	84
1964	635	347	222	66	4215	3204	933	78
1965	373	243	99	31	2337	1764	498	75
1966	232	151	60	21	1948	1430	454	64
1967	217	120	64	33	1109	734	332	43
Total	2575	1410	866	299	15677	11565	3705	407
Cyprus								
1962	164	83	67	14	334	255	63	16
1963	226	84	115	27	474	348	102	24
1964	180	47	89	44	399	259	121	19
1965	78	23	42	13	440	293	133	14
1966	133	50	47	16	373	247	117	9
1967	98	37	58	3	331	231	90	10
Total	859	324	418	117	2351	1633	626	92
Rest of Commonwealth								
1962	1585	598	668	319	4792	2971	1369	452
1963	3064	1194	1263	607	6946	4169	2102	675
1964	2311	873	1003	435	7486	4615	2288	583
1965	1321	516	575	230	5714	3381	1898	435
1966	1031	453	448	130	5907	3727	1901	279
1967	852	432	326	94	5096	3184	1655	257
Total	10164	4066	4283	1815	35941	22047	11213	2681
All Coloured Commonwealth Countries								
1962	3333	1392	1348	593	11101	7484	2914	703
1963	6575	2679	2666	1230	16370	10742	4567	1061
1964	5192	2099	2161	932	18044	11718	5377	949
1965	2973	1310	1181	482	12382	7591	4107	684
1966	2315	1098	944	273	12407	7686	4249	472
1967	1928	958	728	242	9545	5896	3210	439
Total	22316	9536	9028	3752	79849	51117	24424	4308

Voucher Holders			Dependants				Others for Settlement			
Total Persons No.	Men No.	Women No.	Total Persons No.	Men No.	Women No.	Children No.	Total Persons No.	Men No.	Women No.	Children No.
697	439	258	1160	37	426	697	644	109	325	210
754	460	294	2374	83	773	1518	460	66	240	154
1382	885	497	3584	108	920	2556	678	107	338	233
1774	988	786	3667	129	753	2785	327	83	171	73
391	198	193	3256	52	493	2711	264	54	84	126
395	267	128	3339	32	403	2904	270	49	100	121
5393	3237	2156	17380	441	3768	13171	2643	468	1258	917
635	601	34	886	15	714	157	242	26	167	49
1391	1315	76	2292	29	1881	382	124	17	86	21
824	791	33	2492	39	2057	396	92	19	59	14
280	257	23	2452	36	1914	502	66	20	34	12
62	56	6	1882	24	1322	536	84	24	43	17
34	29	5	1103	23	618	462	96	19	55	22
2704	2527	177	11107	166	8506	2435	704	125	444	135
162	108	54	438	17	173	248	333	38	145	150
610	431	179	1063	55	455	553	167	27	54	86
539	347	192	1750	107	600	1043	140	41	46	53
274	137	137	1128	91	492	545	142	43	69	30
80	40	40	587	39	255	293	118	31	40	47
96	49	47	505	34	222	249	103	28	44	31
1761	1112	649	5471	343	2197	2931	1003	208	398	397
783	545	238	1096	21	468	607	904	190	369	345
2708	2117	591	3288	82	1407	1799	736	204	304	228
2766	2086	680	4219	132	1670	2417	845	295	286	264
2270	1572	698	4940	241	1823	2876	638	282	237	119
1217	934	283	4107	120	1561	2426	524	227	170	127
1027	724	303	3936	114	1500	2322	613	223	204	186
10771	7978	2793	21586	710	8429	12447	4260	1421	1570	1269
4217	3123	1094	8220	235	3762	4223	4008	577	1941	1490
28678	26603	2075	24459	773	10516	13170	2934	586	1341	1034
13888	11355	2533	35738	1186	12681	21871	3214	776	1489	949
12125	9326	2799	39228	1419	13965	23844	2297	803	1071	423
5141	4137	1004	39130	1327	12109	25694	2331	858	756	717
4716	3807	907	50083	2098	13216	34769	2849	1058	917	848
68765	58351	10414	196858	7038	66249	123571	17633	4684	7488	5461

Appendix 4 / Immigrant Voucher Holders in 1967

The number of vouchers which were issued to Commonwealth immigrants in 1967 was 8,500, but only 4,978 were actually taken up. Of these, 2,590 were to persons professionally qualified, as follows:

Doctors	938
Dentists	41
Nurses	148
Professions connected with medicine (e.g. physiotherapists, radiographers, etc.)	29
Teachers	565
Scientists	246
Civil Engineers	147
Other Engineers	276
Agricultural Scientists	81
Lawyers	29
Architects	31
Miscellaneous (e.g. accountants, economists, statisticians)	59

Source Hansard (16 May 1968).

References

Official Documents

General Register Office, *Census 1961, England and Wales: Birthplace and Nationality Tables* (London, H.M.S.O., 1964); *Commonwealth Immigrants in the Conurbations* (London, H.M.S.O., 1965).

Sample Census 1966, Great Britain, Summary Tables, Birthplaces of the Whole Population (London, H.M.S.O., 1967), Table 6, pp. 29-38.

Registrar General's Quarterly Reports (London, H.M.S.O.).

Registrar General's Quarterly Review of Births, Deaths and Marriages (London, H.M.S.O.).

Home Office, *Commonwealth Immigrants Act, Control of Immigration Statistics for 1962-1967* (London, H.M.S.O., 1963-8).

Central Statistical Office, *East Caribbean Population Census, 1960* (Trinidad and Tobago, C.S.O., 1961-8).

United Nations, *United Nations Demographic Yearbook* (New York).

Books and Articles

Banton, M. P., *White and Coloured* (London, Jonathan Cape, 1959).

Blake, J., *Family Structure in Jamaica* (New York, The Free Press of Glencoe, 1961).

Davison, R. B., 'The Distribution of Immigrant Groups in London', *Race*. Vol. V, No. 2 (October 1963).

Davison, R. B., *Commonwealth Immigrants* (London, O.U.P., for the Institute of Race Relations, 1964).

Davison, R. B., *Black British: Immigrants to England* (London, O.U.P., for the Institute of Race Relations, 1966).

Gish, O., 'Aliens, Old Commonwealth and New Commonwealth Workers', *Race,* Vol. IX, No. 4 (April, 1968).

Hill, C. S., *West Indian Migrants and the London Churches* (London, O.U.P., for the Institute of Race Relations, 1963).

Institute of Race Relations, *Colour and Immigration in the United Kingdom, 1968* (London, Institute of Race Relations Facts Paper, 1968).

Jenner, P. and Cohen, B. G., 'Commonwealth Immigrants and the 1961 Census (10% Sample) – some Problems in Analysis' (unpublished paper, 1967).

Kelsall, R. K., *Population, the Social Structure of Modern Britain* (London, Longmans and Green, 1967).

Labour Party, *Talking Points,* No. 21, 'Immigration' (December 1968).

Maunder, M. F., 'The New Jamaican Emigration', *Social and Economic Studies,* Vol. IV, No. 1 (March 1955).

Patterson, S., *Dark Strangers: a Study of West Indians in London* (Harmondsworth, Penguin, 1965).

Peach, G. C. K., 'Under-enumeration of West Indians in the 1961 Census', *Sociological Review,* Vol. XIV, No. 1 (March 1966).

Rex, J., *and* Moore, R., *Race, Community and Conflict* (London, O.U.P., for the Institute of Race Relations, 1967).

Richmond, A. H., *The Colour Problem* (Harmondsworth, Penguin, 1955).

Roberts, G. W., *The Population of Jamaica* (London, O.U.P., 1957).

Stycos, J. M., *and* Back, K. W., *The Control of Human Fertility in Jamaica,* (New York, Cornell University Press, 1964).

Tidrick, G., 'Some Aspects of Jamaican Emigration to the United Kingdom, 1953-1962', *Social and Economic Studies,* Vol. XV, No. 1 (March 1966).

Waterhouse, J. A. H., *and* Brabban, D. H., 'Inquiry into the Fertility of Immigrants', *The Eugenics Review* (April 1964), pp. 7-18.

Wiles, Silvaine, 'Children from Overseas', Institute of Race Relations *News Letter* (June 1968).